TRUE SALVATION WHO HAS IT?

SALVATION BY GRACE THROUGH FAITH

BRO. CALEB F. IWORIE

BLUEPRINT PRESS
INTERNATIONALE

Salvation by Grace Through Faith
Copyright © 2023 by Bro. Caleb F. Iworie

ISBN
978-1-961117-04-4 (Paperback)
978-1-961117-05-1 (eBook)
978-1-961117-33-4 (Hardcover)

Dedication

This Book is dedicated to our Lord Jesus Christ for the furtherance of the Gospel.

TABLE OF CONTENTS

At the cross...

SALVATION
BY GRACE THROUGH
FAITH

A humble, submitted heart, in simplicity,
is what brings you to God.

God dwells in a humble heart, not in education,
it's not in schools, not in theology, seminaries, or
in big titles, not in all these other different places,
not in big words, or not in classical places.

God dwells in human hearts. And the lower
you can break yourself down, the more simple,
you can become greater in the sight of God.

God lives in humility and simplicity!

It's so simple, till the big intelligent people today
stagger right over the top of such simplicity. The
trouble with us is, we try to be adults in God, when
we ought to be babies. God dwells in the center
of humility and simplicity. Not in arrogance.
Don't you never forget all these!

BRO CALEB F. IWORIE

ABOUT THIS BOOK

This book is actually intended to tighten some of the loose end teachings that contradict true Bible principles on our SALVATION belief in the Lord Jesus. As we can notice, many people read from a lineup of different Bible versions and references. And they do that sincerely just trying to catch up with revelations, interpretations and understanding, but unknown to them, somehow reduces the entire context. Therefore all Bible quotations herein are taken from the King James Version of the Bible.

Salvation in Christ should bring us to a turning point. Oh yes, a turnaround in our attitudes, a turning point to our motives and objectives of lives. Truly, it is the grace of God that saves you, God's amazing and unmerited grace. I cannot trust in any merits. We need to change our mindsets, calling upon the name of the Lord and accepting Him as our personal Lord and Savior.

WE MUST FIRST REPENT! For whosoever shall call upon the name of the Lord shall be saved. But then, if you are just calling or confessing Him with your lips, by merely giving Him "lip-services" It wouldn't do you any good because faith without works is dead. You must bring forth evidence of true repentance. **There is one thing you must know; you have got to be in Christ or you're**

dead. No matter what the world has to say about you, work to please God!

And if you actually believe that Jesus is the Son of God, how come that you seem to have willingly continued to live the same life you once lived, and yet claiming that you are saved? Even though Salvation is by Grace, Salvation is not by disgrace! Because as a proof that you have been saved. Matt.3:8-10. Bring ye forth therefore fruits meet for repentance: And think not to say within yourselves, we have Abraham to *our* father: for I say unto you, that God is able of these stones to raise up children unto Abraham. And now also **the axe is laid unto the root of the trees: therefore every tree which bringeth not forth good fruit is hewn down, and cast into the fire.** Of course, it is not by our works of righteousness but by His grace alone. Then shall we continue in sin that grace may abound? God forbid! Rom. 6:1. Where is the evidence of His resurrection? If any be in Christ he is a new creation and behold, old things are passed away and all things are come new. If we pattern our lives after the lives of them that believe not, what is the difference? We are supposed to be living epistle read by all men.

Ye are the salt of the earth: but if the salt have lost his savor, wherewith shall it be salted? it is thenceforth good for nothing, but to be cast out, and to be trodden under foot of men.

14 Ye are the light of the world. A city that is set on a hill cannot be hid.

[15] Neither do men light a candle, and put it under a bushel, but on a candlestick; and it giveth light unto all that are in the house.

[16] Let your light so shine before men, that they may see your good works, and glorify your Father which is in heaven. Matthew 5:13-16. To 'be salt' means to deliberately seek to influence the people in one's life by showing them the unconditional love of Christ through good deeds. Light is a symbol used to mean awareness, knowledge, and understanding.

AUTHOR'S NOTE

Now how are we saved? By faith? By works? By a combination of the two?

I say, "By faith through grace believing and resting our faith upon His redemptive works. Every true, genuine, gift of God will point you to the Cross at Calvary, yea to the finished work of the Lord Jesus Christ. There is no one who can heal you; there is no one who can save you; and there is no one who can add one thing to your salvation, yea not a person! But only the Lord Jesus Christ!

What any minister could do would be to preach salvation in Christ Jesus. No preacher can tell you he can save you. He will only introduce Christ to you and ask you to accept the redemptive work that the Lord Jesus has already done for you. Every true minister of our Great God is charged with the responsibility of leading sinners to Christ: - leading the **true** sons and daughters who are already saved from the foundation of the world of God to Christ. That's exactly right Therefore w**e ought to come to Church with the highest degree of reverence and soberness. We ought to godly enter the Church like real saints of God, walk over and take our positions, and keep our minds only focus on Christ. It is not a place to exchange greetings with one another, or a**

show of our new dresses, nor a place to make or solicit for alms or make business contacts. What will Jesus do today if he were to physically come into many of our churches? He did it before and will do it all over again. Whip the people and overturn their tables. "And Jesus went into the temple of God, and cast out all them that sold and bought in the temple, and overthrew the tables of the moneychangers, and the seats of them that sold doves, **13** and said unto them, It is written, My house shall be called the house of prayer; but ye have made it a den of thieves". **Matt. 21:12**

And if you are really born of the Spirit of God, then that is where your heart lays anyhow. Jesus said, "He that heareth My words and believeth on Him that sent Me, has Everlasting Life. And I say again, if you are just confessing Him with your "lips", by pretentiously carrying on, or just giving Him "lip-services", it would not do you any good. But truly from your heart, if you believe that Jesus is the Son of God, then you cannot continue to live the same worldly life you once lived.

Yes, you cannot, if you ever have the true view of Calvary. And, if you are taking your confession in a haphazard way, you are just fooling and deceiving yourself. But if you truly get a view of Who Jesus Is, and what He did for mankind, your heart will rend and tear apart within you. Why don't you desire to throw away all the trash of the world and live for Him alone? Oh, how marvelous that will be! "Come now, and let us reason together, saith the LORD: though your sins be as scarlet, they shall be as white as snow; though they be red like crimson, they shall be as wool. If ye be willing and obedient, ye shall eat the good of the land: But if ye refuse and rebel, ye shall be devoured with the sword: for the mouth of the LORD hath spoken it". Isaiah 1:18-20

Be it known to you that, God Himself, stooped so low, condescended and unfolded Himself, to redeem mortal man till He could get into your heart and giving man abundant life.

Now let me say this to you my sinner friend. You may be reading this book as a prostitute; you may also be promiscuous and an adulterer still reading this book, or as a drunkard, or a gambler, or a murderer. You might even be the vilest of sinners. There is still hope for you!

The decision is yours if you can just repent, confess and believe the gospel, the grace of God will make a way for you in this darkest hour by you accepting it. Adam had to be willing to accept Him to rule over your life.

PREFACE

This book publication will be one of the most intriguing paradoxes in my life as with open eyes; we see the unveiling of our second publication debut targeted at bringing lost souls to Christ, and attempting to *breaking through the New York Times Best Sellers category. And this gospel of the Kingdom will be preached to the uttermost part of the world, and then, the end will come.*

I beseech you therefore by the mercies of our Great Jehovah God, to keep praying fervently without ceasing, for the peace of Jerusalem, and for those who are caught up in hatred death in the Middle East, for the cause of the gospel; both Arab nations, Africa and around the world. Thousands of our Palestinian Christian brethren need our prayers as they personally witness the buildup of holocaust towards Armageddon. *Looking for that blessed hope and glorious appearing of our Lord Jesus Christ.*

How our hearts bleed, as we warn you to, "run for your safety, run for your life to the Christ of the Bible. REPENT of your sins (unbelief) and then line up with His Word: so you might escape the deception and damnation of this evil age in which we live". B*e ye also ready for in such an hour as ye think not the Son of man cometh." Matt. 24:44.*

THE FALL OF MAN WAS A PERMISSIVE WILL

Did you know that it was God's permissive will for SIN to come into this world? Strange, but true.

He permitted sin in order for Him to display His great attributes of being a SAVIOR and a REDEEMER. He allowed Adam and Eve, our first parent, to be deceived by the serpent in order to make way for His great redemptive plan of salvation. God Himself wanted to be glorified. He could not have been glorified as a Savior if there was nobody to be saved in the first place. There had to be sinners first, before He could ever display His attributes of being a Savior.

In the same manner that He had to create sons and daughters in me and you first, so that He could become a Father. Man's existence and fall, therefore, had made God both Father and Savior to us, and a Blessed Redeemer, too.

If you are a true child of God, you are foreknown of God even before there ever was a star or moon in the entire universe. Jesus said, "All that the Father has given Me will come to Me and NONE of THEM will be LOST." The Bible says, "All things work together for good to them that love God", and that "the footsteps of the righteous are ordered by the Lord." Surely, you have to recognize yourself today whether you are God's predestinated or not, for if God has elected you to eternal life, "nothing can pluck you from out of His hand."

GOD'S FOREKNOWLEDGE/ PREDESTINATION

Ephesians 1:5-6 states that God hath "predestinated us according to the good pleasure of His will, to the praise and glory of His grace."

Romans 8:30 further emphasizes this election saying, "Whom He did predestinate, THEM He also called; and whom He called, THEM He also justified; and whom He justified, THEM He also glorified" (past tense). And "their names were written in the Lamb's Book of Life before the foundation of the world" (Rev.13:8)

If you are a true child of God, you are foreknown of God even before there ever was a star or moon in the entire universe. Jesus said, "All that the Father has given Me will come to Me and NONE of THEM will be LOST." The Bible says, "All things work together for good to them that love God", and that "the footsteps of the righteous are ordered by the Lord." Surely, you have to recognize yourself today whether you are God's predestinated or not, for if God has elected you to eternal life, "nothing can pluck you from out of His hand."

Now, who could be saved by the law? No one could be saved by the law. The law didn't come to save us. The law was to magnify our sins, to point them out to us. And listen, to you legalist believers, I want to ask you something: There's not one thing you can do to be saved in yourself. No sir. You are saved by grace and that alone, and you have nothing to do with it. God chose you in Christ before the foundation of the world. That's right.

There's not one thing you can do to merit. So you keep all the commandments you want to, join all the churches you want to, you're still lost. You might know your catechism, say Hail Mary's. You might know the Apostles Creed, the Doxology; you might know all the doctrine of the Bible. But to know the Bible is not Life. To know the church creed is not Life. But to know Him is Life.

You might be baptized this way, that way, this way, that way, or sprinkled, poured, whatever it may be; you're still lost until you know Him. To know Him is Life.

Did you know that it was God's permissive will for SIN to come into this world? Strange, but true. He permitted sin in order for Him to display His great attributes of being a SAVIOR and a REDEEMER. He allowed Adam and Eve, our first parent, to be deceived by the serpent in order to make way for His great redemptive plan of salvation. God Himself wanted to be glorified. He could not have been glorified as a Savior if there was nobody to be saved in the first place. There had to be sinners first, before He could ever display His attributes of being a Savior.

In the same manner that He had to create sons and daughters in me and you first, so that He could become a Father. Man's existence and fall, therefore, had made God both Father and Savior to us, and a Blessed Redeemer, too.

In order to be God, He knew from the very beginning who will be saved and who will not be saved. God was not willing that anyone should perish, but that all might come to repentance.

But He, being infinite, knew the end from the beginning. And therefore, He knew who would accept and those who would not accept His provided way of salvation. He knew who would go to heaven and those who would go to hell. If He didn't, then He isn't God.

But God is unlimited. He is infinite and He makes no mistakes. His works are perfect; and He knows all things. He is the Alpha and Omega, the beginning and the end.

JESUS DIED ONLY FOR THE ELECT

God sent Jesus Christ for only one specific purpose: and that's to save and redeem those who God foreknew will be saved; and not the rest of the world.

Notice Jesus in His prayer to the Father in John 17:9-10, "I pray for them: I pray NOT for the world, but for THEM which Thou hast given Me; for they are Thine. And all Mine are Thine, and Thine are Mine, and I am glorified in THEM."

To "REDEEM" simply means to "TAKE BACK, TO BRING BACK TO IT'S ORIGINAL PLACE" what was originally God's own. Jesus, as a Redeemer, was to take back only those who once belonged originally to God but were trapped in sin by the natural birth. Jesus shed His precious Blood only for those who had been foreknown of God, and for those whose names were written in the Lamb's Book of Life before the foundation of the world. Jesus could never redeem the Devil's children, for they are not of God. They were simply predestinated unto eternal damnation, and were basically created for that purpose. Yes, though this might seem to be a hard saying, but the Scriptures support this truth.

HOW CAN THE POT SAY TO THE POTTER?

Don't you realize that even sinners and reprobates are predestinated by God? Yes, In 1 Peter 2:8 and it says, "Even to them which stumble at the Word, being disobedient: whereunto they were appointed." Jude 1:4 says it, too: "Who were before of old ordained to this condemnation, ungodly men, turning the grace of God into lasciviousness".

Talk about Judas, Cain, Pharaoh and Balaam - all these men had played their significant part as God's adversary in God's greatest drama series, the Bible, without them even realizing it so. "How can the POT say to the POTTER, 'Why hast Thou made me thus?' Hath not the Potter power over the clay to make one vessel unto honour, and another unto dishonour?" (Romans 9:21), these words pertain to predestination. God raises evil to fulfill his glorious purpose of greater good. God said in Isaiah 45:7- "I form the light, and create darkness: I make peace, and create evil: I the LORD do all these things."

THE GOSPEL IS HID TO THEM THAT ARE LOST

Jesus rejoiced in the Spirit (Luke 10:21) saying, "I thank Thee Father, O Lord of heaven and earth, for Thou hast HID these things from the eyes of the wise and prudent, and hast revealed them unto babes; even so, Father, for so it seemed good in Thy sight." This blessed Gospel is, therefore, revealed only to His elected ones. God hid His truth from unbelievers.

Did you know also that one of God's permissive will has been to allow sickness to afflict mankind? Yes, He sometimes permit sickness and diseases in order for Him to manifest Himself as a Healer. Exodus 16:26 states, "For I am the Lord that healeth thee". Isaiah 53:5 states this also: "He was wounded for our transgressions, He was bruised for our iniquities, the chastisement of our peace was upon Him, and by His stripes, we are HEALED". Doctors simply make the stitches and give us prescriptions, but it's still God Who does the real Healing, which is multiplication of new cells in the body, which is creation by nature.

God truly foreordained all His godly attributes to be displayed unto men and all these attributes were finally fulfilled when God Himself became MAN through His Son Jesus Christ and took the penalty for our sins so that by believing in Him we may be justified and forgiven. Jesus said, "I am the way, the truth and the life; no man cometh unto the Father except by Me."

WHO DID CAIN MARRY? ADAM AND EVE HAD THEIR CHILDREN IN EDEN.

When Adam and Eve had their children in Eden, was there other people on earth at this time?

Now read on carefully in Genesis the 5th chapter and the 16th verse, we read "Cain dwelt in the land of Nod and knew his wife".

The salient question is, "who was Cain's wife or who did Cain marry?"

Cain had a wife, because the Bible said he did. And if Cain had a wife, he had to get her somewhere. And as we read on, this would line right into it here: Were there other people on the earth when Adam and Eve had their children in Eden?

If you notice carefully, in the Bible it's ever not recorded about a woman being born. It's always the man child is the one that's recorded in the Bible, not the woman. Seldom is it ever mentioned about the birth of a girl baby, in the Bible. Or, frankly, I don't know as I can recall one right straight off now, in mind, where it ever recorded the birth of a baby girl said, "They begot sons and daughters." lease read on!

Now, the Bible only gives record of three children being born to Adam and Eve, and that was CAIN, ABEL, and SETH.

And, if all three of those being man, and if there wasn't ever any females born, and then when the only female (Eve) died, the human race would have ceased to exist right then, because there'd been no way for them to have the continuity of the human race to have furthered, because there would have been no females left.

Eve would have been the only one. But, you see, they don't record the births of girl babies, in the Bible, therefore they had to have girls the same as boys.

The old writer, one of the most ancient writers we got, Josephus, claims they had seventy children, and Adam and Eve; one of the oldest writers, "seventy children, and they were both sons and daughters."

And then if Cain went to the land of Nod... now, if you notice, the writer made a very, very brilliant writing here. Did you notice how he quoted it? In Eden, when they had their children in Eden...

Now, not in the Garden of Eden, because, the writer knew that. Ever who, wrote the note here, said: when Adam and Eve had their children in Eden...

Not in the Garden of Eden, because they' d been driven out of the Garden of Eden. But they were still in Eden, and the Garden of Eden laid east in Eden. But Eden was like a county or what or a state, and then Nod was another state or county next to it.

Watch closely, now, the only person that Cain could have had, or married, would have had to be his own sister. He had to. Because there's only one male and female that they could have come from, see, and he had to marry his own sister. Now, that was legal in those days.

And Isaac married his own first blood cousin, Rebekah, ordained of God. Sarah was Abraham's sister, his blood sister; not by his mother, by his father. See, a blood sister that Abraham married; a different mother, but same father.

So, you see, to marry in relation then, before the stream of blood was weakened in the human race, it was legal and all right. But now it isn't. If you'd marry your sister today, and have children, they'd probably be deformed. Even down to a first and second cousin should never be married, see, because the bloodstream becoming low and running low.

But the only thing then that Cain could have done, would been, to marry his own sister. And that's where the children was that.

He got his wife, when he went to the land of Nod and knew her, and from there come the children. See?

And if you notice, out of the lineage of Cain come the smart man. And out of the lineage of Seth come the religious man, I mean, the vine of righteousness. Right there, those two, brought forth the very line that we're living in today.

And if you'll notice now: that lineage of Cain still exists, and the lineage of Seth still exists.

They both come down just the same. Cain's children is here amongst us, and Seth's children is here amongst us. As the bloodstream weakens and goes out, but that lineage still hangs on. Oh, amen!

Now, watch. Cain's children were always here before the antediluvian destruction, they were the smart people: the scientist, the educators; and very religious, but was the condemned bunch. See? Now watch, they were just like their father Cain.

Cain, was a religious man. He built a beautiful altar, and made a beautiful church, and tried to make it look prettier than that little mission that Seth had down there. Did you know that?

He decorated the altar with flowers, and fixed it beautiful, and made it pretty; and made a great, big, swell cathedral church, because he thought that he could find favor with God by doing so.

And Abel went over and got a little lamb, and started pulling it over to the altar, and laid it on a rock and killed it.

And now, if God being just, if all He required was worship, Cain worshipped God with just as much sincerity as Abel did. Both of them were sincere. Both of them were trying to find grace with God. They were neither one of them infidel. They were both, absolutely, believers in Jehovah. Now, there, that gives us something to think of.

No matter how religious you are, that doesn't have one thing to do with it. You might live in church, you might be ever so sincere, and you're still lost! See?

And you say, "Well, our pastors are the smartest, they come through the seminaries to get the best education. They're theologians, they know all the theologies and so forth. And they're smart, trained, got DD, Phd, Xyz, the very reverend, the elected best that we know of." And they could still be lost! See?

Now Cain, on his lineage: they were, every one, very religious; a very famous people; and they were scientists, and doctors, and builders, and workers, and smart man. But all that lineage was rejected, from Cain all the way down.

And on Abel's side: they weren't builders nor educators or smart man; they were a, more or less, humble, sort of sheep raisers, and peasants, that just walked by the Spirit.

Now, the Bible said, "There's no condemnation to them that's in Christ Jesus, that walk not after the flesh but after the Spirit." The spiritual man has a spiritual soul that can never die. And the carnal man has a religious atmosphere around him (and wants to worship and so forth) but is carnal; not an unbeliever, but a carnal believer; and it was the kind was rejected.

Now, from there, Cain went and married his wife in the land of Nod. Now, it doesn't say who Seth married, or who others married. And the very beautiful thing of that is to know that, Cain marrying, we have the answer to it. Cause he had to marry his sister. Because there was no more women on the earth, but just had to come from Eve.

She was the mother of all living. That's, all the people that was living, she was the mother of it. That's the reason that she was... The word Eve means "the mother of the living." So she came and brought this child. And Cain married his own sister, would be the only way that I could see out of it. So there was people living in that day, truly. See?

When Adam and Eve had their children in Eden... Now watch, that's the question: WHEN THEY HAD THEIR CHILDREN IN EDEN, WAS THERE OTHER PEOPLE ON EARTH AT THIS TIME? No!

Then in Genesis 5:16, you see, Cain dwelt in the land of Nod and knew his wife. Sure. See?

That's Genesis 1, where He created man in His Own image, which was in the theophany. And in Genesis 2, He made man out of the dust of the earth, which was the human man that we have now.

And then, in 3 was the fall, and was kicked out from the Garden of Eden; and then the children begat children. And Cain took his wife and lived with her in the land of Nod, outside, because God had separated him from the fellowship with his own brother (because of the death of Abel).

And that's who he had, his own sister, and married her; is the only way that I can, myself, can see how that he married.

THE HOLY BIBLE, WHAT A WORD, WHAT A BOOK!

I just don't believe God would leave us down here without a copy of His Word for our guidance.

And only a few professing Christians realize what they have in their possession, in a Book called The Holy Bible. For the Bible is the Absolute FINAL AUTHORITY to settle all questions concerning Christian Conduct, Church Order, And Doctrine. Realizing that we will be ultimately judged by what is written in God's Word, it's important that we 'line-up' with it. Jesus Said, "If ye continue in my Word, then are ye my disciples indeed;" John 8:31.

For thousands of years, Man has tried to prove his height, his depth, his breadth still we are only scratching the surface of its richness. So enduring is the Word of God, as contained in the pages of the Bible that Jesus said, "Heaven and earth shall pass away, but my words shall not pass away." Matthew 24:35.

Christianity is the only established channel upon which has the writings of a Book as unique as that of The Holy Bible - the Words of which are with POWER - life-changing, life-sustaining Power - Eternal Life! "Christianity is based upon the impregnable Rock of Holy

Scriptures." The very foundation upon which Christian truth rests is the reality of the Divine Inspiration of the Bible. For the True Christian, the Bible is the FINAL SUPREME COURT OF APPEAL in all matters.

And as it is written, in 2 Timothy 3:16-17 KJV

[16]All scripture is given by inspiration of God and is profitable for doctrine, for reproof, for correction, for instruction in righteousness:

[17] That the man of God may be perfect, thoroughly furnished unto all good works. Again as it is written, in 2 Peter 1:21 KJV. For the prophecy came not in old time by the will of man: but holy men of God spake as they were moved by the Holy Ghost. See?

The Bible in itself is the most amazing Book. No other book ever was written has ever had an impact on mankind as this book. No other book has ever been studied and read as much as the Holy Bible. No other book has been reproduced as much as this Bible, and no other book has been more controversial. What a Word, What a Book!

Other books have been controversial in its season' but after those books are forgotten and lost in time, the Bible still remains, is still printed by the millions, is still read, still discussed, still controversial, and still having an impact upon the world - clear evidence according to Hebrews 4:12 KJV that: For the word of God is quick, and powerful, and sharper than any two-edged sword, piercing even to the dividing asunder of soul and spirit, and of the joints and marrow, and is a discerner of the thoughts and intents of the heart.

Isaiah 66:2 KJV

[2] For all those things hath mine hand made, and all those things have been, saith the Lord: but to this man will I look, even to him that is poor and of a contrite spirit, and trembleth at my word.

John 5:24 KJV. Verily, verily, I say unto you, He that heareth my word, and believeth on him that sent me, hath everlasting life, and shall not come into condemnation; but is passed from death unto life.

John 8:31 KJV. Then said Jesus to those Jews which believed on him, If ye continue in my word, then are ye my disciples indeed;

Psalms 119:89. Forever, O Lord, thy word is settled in heaven.

Matthew 4:4. Man shall not live by bread alone but by every word that proceedeth out of the mouth of God.

To further establish the Authority of the Bible, God ordained that these words be penned near the end of the last chapter of The Book of Revelation... 22:18 For I testify unto every man that heareth the words of the prophecy of this book, If any man shall add unto these things, God shall add unto him the plagues that are written in this book:

22:19 And if any man shall take away from the words of the book of this prophecy, God shall take away his part out of the book of life, and out of the holy city, and from the things which are written in this book.

Therefore, to the Christian, the Word of God as contained in the Bible is the Absolute and Final Authority to settle all questions concerning Christian Conduct, Church

Order, And Doctrine. Realizing that we will be ultimately judged by what's written in God's Word, it's important that we line-up' with it. Jesus Said, "If ye continue in my Word, then are ye my disciples indeed;" John 8:31.

PSALM 119:89-96 KJV.

[89] FOREVER, O LORD, THY WORD IS SETTLED IN HEAVEN.

[90] Thy faithfulness is unto all generations: thou hast established the earth, and it abideth.

[91] They continue this day according to thine ordinances: for all are thy servants.

[92] Unless thy law had been my delights, I should then have perished in mine affliction.

[93] I will never forget thy precepts: for with them, thou hast quickened me.

[94] I am thine, save me: for I have sought thy precepts.

[95] The wicked have waited for me to destroy me: but I will consider thy testimonies

[96] I have seen an end of all perfection: but thy commandment is exceeding broad.

THE RAPTURE/ TRANSLATION OF THE SAINTS: PREPARE TO MEET THY GOD!

Now how many believe that there is going to be the translation of the Saints or the rapture of the Church? You better believe it! The Rapture is for a people who have been purged and prepared to rule and reign during the millennium. And right after this event, shall the great tribulation set in and burn the earth. Oh, how our hearts bleed because multitudes will literally worship the antichrist. But as the lightning cometh from the east unto the west, so shall the coming of the Son of man be.

THERE EXIST SIX RAPTURES IN THE BIBLE:

Notice, four out of the six recorded Raptures have taken place already and there are yet two more raptures to come. Three of them took place in the Old Testament.

The FIRST RAPTURE was when ENOCH was caught away to heaven before the Flood came in Noah's days Gen 5:24.

The SECOND RAPTURE was when ELIJAH was taken away alive in a chariot of fire 2Kings 2:11. leaving his mantle to Elisha.

The THIRD RAPTURE was when the Old Testament Saints Abraham, Sarah, Isaac, Jacob, Joseph, and others rose up from the dead at the time when Jesus shouted with a loud voice at the Cross of Calvary. The graves of those saints were opened and their glorified bodies arose and appeared unto many. Matt. 27:50-53

Jesus, when he had cried again with a loud voice, yielded up the ghost. And, behold, the veil of the temple was rent in twain from the top to the bottom; and the earth did quake, and the rocks rent; and the graves were opened; and many bodies of the saints which slept arose, and came out of the graves after his resurrection, and went into the holy city, and appeared unto many."

In order for these Old Testament Saints to be transported beyond the curtain of time, their sins had to be totally blotted out. The blood of bulls and goats in the Old Testament never had the power to do that. It just covered their sins temporarily and they always had to offer a sacrifice every year in order to maintain their cleanliness before God. They had to wait for that "Perfect Sacrifice" to come, the "Lamb of God" Himself who takes away the sins of the world. Jesus' precious Blood finally released them from the guilt of sin. Mankind's entire sin problem was settled when Jesus died on the cross. Jhn 3:16.

The FOURTH RAPTURE took place when our Lord Jesus Christ himself finally ascended up into the heavens, as it is written in Acts 1:9 to 11. And when he had spoken these things, while they beheld, he was taken up; and a cloud received him out of their sight. And while they looked steadfastly toward heaven as he went up, behold, two men stood by them in white apparel; which also said, Ye men of Galilee, why stand ye gazing up into heaven? This same Jesus, who is taken up from you into heaven, shall so come in like manner as ye have seen him go into heaven."

The FIFTH RAPTURE is that which is spoken of in 1Thess 4:1618 and 1Cor 15:51-54, which concerns all the true believing born Christians who had lived from the Day of Pentecost till this day. All these saints are bound to meet the Lord in the air comes rapture time. They are the ones who are spoken of in "the dead in Christ shall rise first: Then we which are alive and remain (in the Faith once delivered unto the Saints) shall be caught up together with them in the clouds, to meet the Lord in the air".

Only the wise virgins are considered in this FIFTH RAPTURE. These are those who have received "OIL" in their lamps, which is the "Baptism of the Holy Ghost," by heeding to and believing the evening time message of their day to go in the Rapture.

Hundreds and hundreds of denominational people coming in, seeking the Holy Ghost. Don't you know Jesus said when the sleeping virgin come to buy oil, it was that very hour that the Bridegroom come? When she comes, and said, "Let us have some of your oil," said, "We just have enough for ourselves. Go buy." And when she went to buy the oil (the sleeping virgin) then the Bridegroom comes and the Bride went in. Now, there's never been a time that we've ever known that the denominational world has been wanting the Holy Ghost until right now.

The SIXTH RAPTURE will transpire when the Two Witnesses (Moses and Elijah) of Revelation 11 will have come to Israel to call out the 144,000 Jews back to the Gospel of Jesus Christ.

Remember that the Jews were blinded to this truth until the fullness of the Gentiles be fulfilled. Moses and Elijah will come to Israel to testify to them about Jesus Christ being their true Messiah. They will show signs and wonders following their earlier ministry. The Antichrist will hate these two prophets and will kill them, but God will raise them up again after three days and be caught up into Heaven. Make no mistake about it. Here it is written in Revelation 11:3-12:

"And I will give power unto my two witnesses, and they shall prophesy a thousand two hundred and threescore days, clothed in sackcloth. These are the two olive trees, and the two candlesticks standing before the God of the earth. And if any man will hurt them, fire proceedeth out of their mouth, and devoureth their enemies: and if any man will hurt them, he must in this manner be killed.

These two have the power to shut Heaven that it rain not in the days of their prophecy (Elijah): and have power over waters to turn them to blood, and to smite the earth with all plagues, as often as they will (Moses).

And when they shall have finished their testimony, the beast that ascendeth out of the bottomless pit shall make war against them, and shall overcome them, and kill them. And their dead bodies shall lie in the street of the great city, which spiritually is called Sodom and Egypt, where also our Lord was crucified. And they of the people and kindreds and tongues and nations shall see their dead bodies three days and a half, and shall not suffer their dead bodies to be put in graves. And they that dwell upon the earth shall rejoice over them, and make merry, and shall send gifts one to another; because these two prophets tormented them that dwelt on the earth.

And after three days and a half, the Spirit of life from God entered into them, and they stood upon their feet, and great fear fell upon them which saw them. And they heard a great voice from heaven saying unto them, Come up hither. And they ascended up to heaven in a cloud, and their enemies beheld them.

We are living in the shadows of time. We are living in a borrowed time. Time is no longer on our side. Time up, brothers and sisters, hurry, and prepare to meet your Maker!

REPENT NOW, AND BELIEVE THE GOSPEL

*F*or if there is no repentance, then judgment is sure to come! Hezekiah repented. See? Nineveh repented. But Ahab never repented, Jezebel never repented; Nebuchadnezzar never repented, Judas also never repented. The people in Noah's time never repented, and the judgment swept right on them. but Peter repented. See? Now, God always first warns everybody. Everybody gets a warning. Repent or you perish. Lk 13:3-5

Now, seeing the time is at hand, let everyone that feels that there is a warning, repent quickly before the wrath of God strikes.

Now, an apostate or reprobate is someone that has heard the truth and after receiving all the facts then decided to turn it down for something that was more into his fashion and rejected the very truth he once believed. That is an apostate. It has nothing to do with sinners out there. They have a better chance.

The Bible said in Hebrew 6:4-6, "For it's impossible for those who were once enlightened, and have tasted of the heavenly gift, and were made partakers of the Holy Ghost.... If they shall fall away, to renew them again to repentance;

seeing they crucify to themselves the Son of God afresh and put him to an open shame." It is exactly right. Sinners can repent and come to God, but not the apostate.

Repent and believe the gospel, do not harden your heart for God is not willing that any should perish but that you come to repentance.

And **gifts and callings are the predestination of God.** *They are even without repentance.* **You are born with it.** *And that can pull you over and make you think you are saved yet performing great signs and wonder. That gift can lead you to hell if you neglect to be led and directed by the word and, because you cannot step on the pedal. See? God must operate it. You must get yourself out of the way. You believe with all your heart that Jesus Christ lives today.* **Luke 10:20 Context.** [17] And the seventy returned with joy, saying, Lord, even the devils are subject unto us through thy name. [18] And he said unto them, I beheld Satan as lightning fall from heaven. [19] Behold, I give unto you power to tread on serpents and scorpions, and over all the power of the enemy: and nothing shall by any means hurt you. [20] Notwithstanding in this rejoice not, that the spirits are subject unto you; but rather rejoice, because your names are written in heaven.

So then gifts and calling without repentance, or no evidence of repentance

Any Bible student knows that is the truth. **Moses was born just in time.** *Jeremiah, in time, all the rest of them. John the Baptist, in time. Jesus was in time. And we are in time. This is what is supposed to happen.*

Matthew. 7:22-23. Many will say to me in that day, Lord, Lord, have we not prophesied in thy name? and in thy name have cast out devils? and in thy name done many wonderful works? And then will I profess unto them, I never knew you: depart from me, ye that work iniquity.

Brother, sister, friend, seeing the time is at hand, let everyone that feels that there is a warning, repent quickly before the wrath of God strikes.

Things change when man meets God.

A man can never meet God and ever remains the same again. You will either be a better person or a worse person. You'll be better off, or worse off after you meet God. It depends on what you want to do about it. But a man can never meet God and ever be the same.

Whatever your attitude is towards God, seals your eternal destination.

You can walk across the line between grace, mercy, and judgment; and when you spurn grace so many times you can separate yourself from ever from the Presence of God, or you can accept Him and have Eternal Life, and never die, but be raised up again at the last day in the general resurrection.

Romans 6:23 For the wages of sin is death; but the gift of God is eternal life through Jesus Christ our Lord.

SALVATION BY GRACE, THROUGH FAITH:

From our study of the New Testament scriptures, and as featured in our debut edition titled Man's Spiritual Reality, we realize that after a man is **justified** from sin {unbelief} by believing unto repentance through Christ's atonement, God promised to **sanctify** that sinner man "with the washing of water by the Word" Eph. 5:26 until he is truly repented and be baptized by immersion in the name of Jesus Christ for the remission of sins. Acts 2:38. Such a person is only believing unto, and not yet born again. Right after this process according to Acts. 2:39, the believer receives the promise of the **Baptism of Holy Ghost, for the promise is unto you**, and to **your children**, and to all that are afar off, even as many as the LORD our God shall call. Herein we see a display of the three works of grace Justification by faith, Sanctification {cleansing or renewal} and the Baptism of the Holy Ghost as the three stages of the Christian growth for dynamics upon our mechanics.

Sadly enough, majority of the preachers today dwell mostly on prosperity, signs and wonders. And many who hear these preachers and receiving these miracles are thinking they have been saved. While some other preachers are bringing the people to the conclusion that Salvation is a '**one-time**' decision to believe in the Lord Jesus by '**intellectually accepting**' Him as your Lord and Savior. And so making them to believe they are now saved or even born again with that "lip service', or wishy-washy mind set. Oh that is 'kuku bingo belief'. Away with that bald and invalid teaching for there is no truth in it. But **Jesus in His own Words in John 8:31-32 disproved the error of this teaching:** *"said Jesus unto those Jews which 'believed' on Him, "If ye continue in my Word, then are ye my disciples indeed; AND ye shall KNOW the Truth, AND the Truth shall set you FREE."* Therefore, in this edition, we would try to tighten all these loose ends of one of the most misunderstood delusion of the modern day Bible theological teachings on "Salvation". To some others, in their teachings and practice, to be born again, and Salvation have both become intellectual slogans; so messed up in such that the apostate teaching of "Grace" produces nothing but a disgrace to Christianity. What and how can? But God is not mocked!

What shall we say then? Shall we continue in sin, that grace may abound? Oh God forbid! How shall we, that are dead to sin, live any longer therein? Rom 6:1-2.

As you will realize, it is not enough to just say it with your lips; but you have to truly show forth that you believe your confession. Many Christians just quote the first part of the verse Eph 2:8: *"By grace are ye save..."* ; *but the full text says,* "By Grace are ye save THROUGH faith" . Therefore, Salvation is *"BY Grace THROUGH faith"* {as a revelation of the will of God to mankind}. *But without faith it is impossible to please Him: for he that cometh to God must believe that He is, and that He is a Rewarder of them that diligently seek Him". Heb 11:6.*

And as we can read, on the day of Pentecost, **Acts 2:37-38**, we realize that "GRACE through Faith" was clearly demonstrated! God by His sovereign Grace had drawn all the people together to hear the preaching of the Word that would give them the Faith (revelation) of Salvation. **Peter preached the revelation of Jesus Christ, to the people and expounded them of the things that God was doing in their day, and what God had already accomplished in the death and resurrection of Jesus Christ. And as always the preaching of the gospel of Jesus convicted the heart and conscience of the predestinated sons and daughters of God. The Bible says ...** *"Now when they heard this,* **they were pricked [convicted] in their heart, and said unto Peter and to the rest of the apostles, men and brethren, "what shall we do"?**

That is the question we all need to find the answer: **"What shall we DO - to be saved**?" Now let us take note of Peter's answer:

"Then Peter answered and said unto them, **'Repent, and be baptized** every one of you in the name of Jesus Christ for the remission of sins, and ye shall receive the gift of the Holy Ghost. For the promise is unto you [Jews], and to your children [Jews], and to all that are afar off [Gentiles], even as many as the Lord our God shall call {**Jews and Gentiles**}. "

GOD'S PLAN OF REDEMPTION FOR MANKIND:

God has so many children. So there will only ever be so many Christians. When the last saint is born-again, God takes them Home to the Wedding Supper, and the world enters the great tribulation. That day is fast approaching.

We are the last generation. There can be no more. Jesus said, that the generation which sees Israel restored to the homeland would not pass away through old age before the millennium. Soon cometh the earthquake, marking the end of the Gentile age. He's patiently waited almost 2,000 years for his wife {The Church} to make herself ready.

If you and I are serious with God, and not just playing Church', we would better realize the lateness of the hour, get up to speed, do our spiritual homework, and search the scriptures to recognize our day and its Message.

You can't rely on me, or your pastor, to do your religion for you. Your minister or kind old priest can't save you. We're responsible to God for what we teach. If it is faith in the present Truth, we must first receive that faith from God. We can preach it to you, and prove it by the Bible, but you must understand and receive it from God, personally. You must prove it in your Bible and take his Word. God is the Word. The Bible is God in the Form of paper and ink, as Jesus was God in the form of a virgin-born Man. We must personally meet God in the Word. For each one of us must work out our own salvation with fear and trembling. God has no grand children. He has sons and daughters.

In our book "Man's Spiritual Reality" we made deposition that the new birth is the baptism of the Holy Ghost. And we discovered that 'seeing' is understanding, or faith. Faith is a clear understanding of the revealed Word of God.

And we paraphrased I John 1:7, which says, 'UNLESS our life is manifesting the present truth God is fulfilling now, we are not, and cannot come under the blood, or be born again'.

We must recognize our day in the Bible and receive its message, or we can't become a part of Christ's body, the true Church. We can only be born of the Word he is fulling now.

Now, what is the promise of God's Word for THIS day? You search the Scripture and write down just what God promised he would do in this day. Except a man is born again he cannot see....{understand} the Kingdom of God.

The new birth is oneness with God. And God is the Word so the only way we can be one with God is to be in agreement with his Word by faith. That is, we must understand His Word, which is to have His mind, or faith.

If we view the new birth as a theologian would teach it we'd speak of three stages of grace. Justification by grace through faith, sanctification by the blood, and the sealing or baptism with the Holy Ghost. These three steps of faith make up the new birth. Grab your copy of our book titled "Man's Spiritual Reality " {the spirit man}.

God redeems his children the same way as he redeems this earth from which our bodies are made. In 2Peter 3:5-13, he refers to three stages of the earth. The old world before the Flood. The present world we live in now, and the new world that's yet to come.

God lays out His plan of redemption so clearly. What He's done to redeem His world is the same plan He's using to redeem his people! For the unchangeable God changes none of His plans.

He's led us to Himself by three stages of grace so He can dwell in us, just as He's taking the world through three stages of grace to purify it so that He can live on earth throughout eternity in His family.

God is perfected in three's. Malachi 3:6 says, 'I am the Lord and I change not'! Therefore, if He saved the first man He ever saved by the shed blood of an innocent one, He will have to save the next one; and everyone He saves the same way. If He healed a man at any time, be it in the days of Jesus, the apostles, whenever it was, when the same conditions are met, He's got to do it again! He doesn't change. Men change, times change, dispensations change, but God remains the same - perfect! What a hope that ought to give sick people.

If ever he healed a person, He has to do it again, when the same conditions are met. If He ever He0 saves a man, He's got to do it on the same grounds He did it the first time. If He ever filled a man with the Holy Ghost, He's got to do it on the same grounds He did the first time. if ever He raised a man from the grave, He must do it the second time and every other time on the same principle. He doesn't change.

What hope that gives us! It's not some man-made theory, but His unchangeable Word!

You say, "Is It the truth?"

He said, 'Let God's Word be true, but every MAN a liar ... heavens and earth will pass away, or change, but My Word shall never fail'.

'All scripture is given by inspiration of God, and is profitable for doctrine'; and remember ALL Scripture will be fulfilled! Every Word of it!

Notice, how God makes it plain to us? 2Peter 3 was a great confirmation how a good loving God redeems man through those three stages of grace!

The first step is a revelation of the true oneness of the Godhead and repentance towards God, followed by water baptism: 'Repent and be baptized in the Name of the Lord Jesus Christ'. Showing that repentance was genuine, and to REMIT our past sin.

That has nothing to do with future sin. It only remits. 'Repent and be baptized in the Name of Jesus Christ'. What for? Remission: the taking away of past sin; has nothing to do with the future.

Only your past sin is remitted - what you have done.

You can't repent for what Adam did. You never did it; Adam did. You're just forgiven for what you've done. The old nature is still there.

If a drawing of two hearts are drawn across board. Here is a human heart, and here is a human heart. One of the drawings over here has a snake in it - that's sin. He has his life. The one over here has a dove in it, which is the Holy Spirit and he has a Life. This first one here has malice, hatred, envy. What's causing it, is this fellow here, the snake. Now this one over here has love, and joy, and long-suffering, and what does it is the dove.

Now, when you repent and are baptized in the Name of Jesus Christ, you're forgiven of your sins. But you've only erased the record of this past malice, hatred, envy, etc., The thing that made you do it is still there. That snake, the old root of evil, it's still there.

Secondly comes sanctification, which sets our mind in order for holiness, to think right. Sanctification is a compound Greek word which means cleaned and set aside for service. But that snake is still there.

Next comes the baptism of the Fire and Holy Ghost so God may dwell in us. The Fire of God cleanses our heart from sin and puts the Holy Ghost inside. The snake is killed. Then we bring forth the same Life this dove did in the other fellow, because that's the Life that's now in us.

If we went down to the fowl yard and picked up a drinking glass or tumbler from the filth and muck. Yuck! It's covered in manure and dirt, you wouldn't drink from it. But that types God calling us, and justification by grace. Next, we'd take that glass and baptize it under water. Then we'd give it a really good cleansing with disinfectant. That types sanctification, making it ready for use. But it's not in use until it's FILLED. And the Bible believer who is justified and sanctified is not in use until he's been filled with the Spirit of God.

That's why Jesus told Peter, 'AFTER you are converted, or FILLED with the spirit, then you can strengthen your brethren'. God never changes. The way He sent Jesus is the way He's sending us. He sent Jesus full of the Spirit, and He won't send us until we are full of the same Spirit. Three stages or steps in grace.

The natural birth types the spiritual birth. In the natural, when a woman gives birth to a baby, the first thing that happens is breaking of water, then blood, and then the shock of cold air or a slap from the doctor spanking the little fellow, and the spirit of life enters and away he goes screaming. Water, blood, spirit. See?

And a Spirit babe is born into the kingdom of God the same way: water, blood, spirit.

Now sanctification, the second stage, cleanses and sets the mind of the heart in order of holiness. 'As a man thinketh in his heart so is he'.

Sanctification only sets him aside for service.

A man can repent of sin and be justified yet still be thinking of, say he's an immoral man. Every immoral-looking woman he sees, that desire is still there. Maybe he's a drunkard. Every time he smells a drink, it's still there. See? But when he's sanctified, that cleanses the desire out of him. It takes the want of it away. He can still be tempted, but the want of it is gone. But he's still not right. Then, he is baptized with the Holy Ghost and Fire; burnt out, cleaned up, and put INTO the service of God.

It is possible for a man to be justified without being sanctified, or sanctified without being justified, and it's possible for him to be justified and sanctified without the baptism of the Holy Ghost, and eventually be lost. I want to prove by Scripture that all three stages are required for the new birth.

Too many of today's ministers take their people to justification and no further. Take the Baptists who teach that we are born again when we believe. The Bible says, you receive the Holy Ghost AFTER you believe' (Acts 19:3; 2:38; Ephesians 1:13). And many others encourage people to speak with tongues WITHOUT receiving the Holy Spirit.

Didn't Jesus say, it would be so close it would almost deceive the very elect if that were possible? He also said many would come in the last days - that's now - and say, 'Lord, Lord, in your Name we spoke in other tongues, healed the sick, and prophesied. And He will say, depart from Me, ye that work iniquity. I never even knew you'.

So don't think the Gifts of the Spirit have anything to do with the new birth. They do NOT. And they NEVER did.

Let's take Judas Iscariot, an apostle chosen by the Lord Jesus. He had the Gifts of the Spirit and no less a part of the ministry than the others. According to John 4:1-2 he was justified by grace through faith and baptized. He was sanctified by the Word of God, and prayer, John 17:17. But he failed to DIE to his own ideas, go ALL the way to Pentecost, and be born-again.

All three stages are required. I John 5:6-10 compares the natural birth with the spiritual birth. 'This is he that came by water and blood, even Jesus Christ; not by water only, but by water and blood. And it is the spirit that beareth witness, because the Spirit is truth. For there are three that bear record or witness in heaven, the father, the

Word, and the Holy Ghost: and these three ARE One. These three witnesses are One God, NOT three Gods.

And there are three witnesses that bear record in earth, the spirit of mortal life, the water, and the blood. These three AGREE in one natural birth. They are NOT one but they make one natural birth.

If we receive the witness of men, the witness of God is greater: for this is the witness of God which he hath testified of his son. He that believeth on the son of God hath the witness in himself..' That's the witness we want in us - the Holy Ghost. And you cannot have the Holy Ghost without having the Father and the Son, because these three are ONE. One God in three major dispensation claims or Offices, not a trinity: God ABOVE His people as Father, God WITH His people as the Son, and God IN His people as the Holy Ghost.

You can be justified and baptized in the Name of the Lord Jesus Christ, and still not be sanctified. You can be sanctified and not justified, and you can be justified and sanctified without the Holy Ghost. All three are required for the Spiritual birth, as they are for the natural birth. These three agree in one. But you can't have the father without having the son and the Holy Spirit because these three are one.

Notice how this came to pass in the corporate Body as God added line upon line, precept upon precept, Word upon Word. The message grew through Martin Luther from justification to John Wesley, whose ministry added sanctification to Luther's revelation; then in the age of the Pentecostals, the baptism of the Holy Ghost was added to them. These three messages comprise the complete birth.

That's why there can't be any more ages. We're at the end time. Three stages. The baptism cleanses the heart with the Holy Ghost.

He's called the Church through justification; called it through sanctification; then filled it with the Holy Ghost and Fire. He took it through this process, so He, the Holy Spirit himself, the Son of God, could dwell in the human heart. He redeems the earth where we'll dwell through the same process of salvation.

Notice the antediluvian world. He gave it a water baptism, covered it over with water in Noah's flood. Typing our justification, and showing that this fallen world is on its way back to a restoration to Eden's innocence again. Then Jesus came and shed his blood upon it, cleansing it and claiming it. Sanctification. But it's still the same old sinful world that we live in now. When He took Jesus upon the mountain, Satan tried to make Him break God's plan of redemption by giving Him this sinful old world without purchase of the blood.

They tried to give Abraham the land, but he bought it for so many shekels of silver before the people as a ensign, a witness: 'Let it be known this day that I've bought this place'! A purchase. And Satan tried to give Jesus the kingdom which belongs to him now. Tried to give it to him as a gift, but Jesus wouldn't receive it, because Satan would still have a claim upon it. It had to be bought!

As Christ called the Church to repentance, and baptism in the Name of Jesus Christ for the remission of sins, sanctification by the blood, and with the Fire of God, burnt out the filth so He could come and dwell in the human heart; this world is to receive its baptism of Fire.

Satan tried to say, `I will give it to you'. He said, `No, sir, I will buy it!' Let it be a witness. He was lifted up for an witness that He bought it; He purchased it. But now it has to go through a baptism of Fire - holy Fire from God which cleanses the earth and the heavens so that the redeemed can live in peace upon it.

The baptism of fire is to cleanse it from sin, from sickness, from disease, germs, from sinners, from the devil and all of his group. They're to be cast out into the Lake of Fire. Holy Fire from God comes down from heaven and burns it up to make it ready for God to dwell in. For in the new world that is to come, God will dwell in the earth.

You say, "God? He dwells in the human heart."

But, He and the Bride become one, and They go to their Home in the new world. And the same plan of redemption is used to redeem both the world and the persons that live in it.

The heart has to be cleansed like that, before God can come in the person of the Holy Ghost, which is Christ, coming to dwell in the human heart. It must first be repentant and baptized in water in His Name (not three of His many Titles) to show Who it belongs to. Then it must be cleansed by the blood of Jesus. Then the holy Fire from God comes and burns out all the desire of sin, all the nature of the world.

Therefore, he who sins willfully after receiving the knowledge of the truth... then again the Bible said it's IMPOSSIBLE, for a man who's born of God cannot sin; he does not sin. There's no way for him to sin. How can he be a sinner and redeemed at the same time? How can I be in the pawn shop and out of the pawn shop at the same time? Oh, He redeemed us by His blood; cleansed us by His spirit, then comes to dwell in us, the Church (not the denomination, the Church).

The antediluvian repentance brought water baptism. Then Christ came and shed His blood upon it to cleanse and to claim it. Next comes the destruction of the world as it is now. All the sin in heavens above ward off blessings from God. Satan is the prince of the power of the air. Thunderbolts of lightning, sheets of ice and rain, typhoons and storms, come from Satan the prince of the power of the air!

It's baptism of fire will cleanse it from all germs, all diseases, all sicknesses even all the spiritual things (as it did for us) to prepare it for God to dwell in, in this great age that's coming, the new earth.

He redeems it in the same way He redeems His people. His plan of redemption is the same. For He's the unchangeable God.

ONLY A TINY GROUP IS GOING TO 3be taken in the days of his coming. Jesus said, `Strait is the gate, and narrow the way, and FEW there be that find it'.

And the Bible says, `As it was in the days of Noah, wherein eight souls were saved by water, so shall it be in the coming'. Remember there were only eight souls in the ark. And Noah types the remnant that's carried over - not the translated Bride.

Enoch, ONE man, went in the rapture before the flood, showing that the elect Church does not go into the tribulation. Oh, the nominal church may be a great number, but compare eight with one. Enoch was translated, ONE man! The Bride will be eight times less than the church. The Bride is going to be a very small group.

'And if the righteous be scarcely saved, where will the sinner and the ungodly appear'? Those who know better than to do it, yet go ahead and do it anyhow, who follow denominational rules INSTEAD of the Word, yet take the Name of Christ and are called Christians. Where will they appear?

Noah was a type of those who go into the tribulation. When Noah came out, Ham was with him. Sin was still in there. Do you see it? Justification alone is NOT the new birth, that old snake is STILL there. PROVEN in this type. Unbelief, went right on over through the ark. But Enoch went higher than the ark! He went on into the Presence of God.

This PROVES that the millennium is not the end of it. There will still be TIME after the millennium, a judgment and disposition of sin. The millennium is a space of time. The new earth is eternity.

The redeemed earth goes back to its original owner again. He takes the earth away from Satan, just like He takes you away from Satan; like He took the little woman at the well away from Satan.

She saw it by faith. She already believed and was looking for this Promise to be fulfilled. 'I know when Messiah comes, He'll have this sign'. Jesus said, 'I am He'. Wow! She was redeemed right there! 'My sheep receive my Word'. She ran into town and started a revival, 'Come see a man who discerned the thoughts and intents of my heart. Isn't this the very Messiah'?

He only came to redeem that which had fallen. And through the Fall this girl became messed up with sin but she, was in God's thinking before the foundation of the world, foreknown as a believer, and he came to pay her debt, and cleanse her of her sins.

What did the priest call him? He had no faith, only intellectual learning. When he saw Jesus discern the thoughts and intents of the heart, he called it 'Beelzebub', a devil! Because that's what his denomination called it. That sent him back to his destination. He was lost. He was not foreknown as having faith. Jesus could NOT redeem him.

Listen, if the only thing you have, is intellectual learning, like that denominational man, you should better get faith. And the only way you will ever have it is if you were foreknown in Christ from the foundation of the world.

From the beginning, God made His way of salvation plain by His prophets. He's never changed it! He justifies a man, sanctifies him, sends the holy Fire to burnt sin out of him, then comes and dwells in him Himself.

He uses the same plan of redemption for the earth. It repented and was baptized in water by Noah. Jesus came and sanctified it by dripping His blood upon it and claiming it. And the new earth to come is to have a holy Fire baptism to clean it of every devil, every germ, every sickness and make it anew.

I saw a new heaven and a new earth'. You become a new person! Amen! Not just the old one patched up by joining church or trying to turn a new page. You are a brand new unit.

God takes the old man and burns him completely out with the Holy Ghost and Fire and moves in Himself. No man can come to Me except My Father has drawn him. And all the Father has given me will come to Me'. You see it? The SAME plan.

Satan will be taken from the earth, just exactly as he was taken from you. Satan can tempt, but cannot deceive a born again Christian. God foresaw him from the foundation of the world, and sent Jesus to redeem him. The blood speaks for him. How can he sin when he can't even be seen? God just sees your representation, Christ! And He hears your voice. Amen!

The world is an attribute of God's thinking, just as the believer is one of his attributes. From the foundation of the world it was in God's mind to have a earth, to be on a throne, to be a king, to be a redeemer, to be a healer; that's his attributes just like you are one of his attributes.

We had to be in the mind of God before there was a world. Before there was an atom or molecule, His elect were IN Him as a thought. His thoughts are eternal, they are real. IF we are God's children, we were ALWAYS in the Logos or Word of God because His Word is His thoughts expressed. That's how Isaiah could say a virgin was going to conceive? That Word of prophecy was God's thoughts expressed by Isaiah's faith.

'Let the mind that was in Christ be in you'. Then what you say is not your idea; it's His thought, and you're expressing His Words. His Words cannot fail. Isaiah said, 'a virgin shall conceive'. That settles it: she's going to conceive. What God says, He does.

By His prophets He makes all of his manifestations known, because they're the attributes of His thoughts expressed. Now this little woman at the well was one of His attributes.

And there was a priest representing the light. He'd learned from the Bible that God was God; he'd learned that holiness was right; and he'd learned the law by intellectual conception. And he was born of the right lineage: he was a Levite, but he only knew it by intellectual conception! And when he met the light of the hour his denomination knew nothing about it. But here was the Redeemer on earth at that time to redeem His attributes - and she received It.

She never questioned it. She said, 'I know, when Messiah comes, He'll do this'. She saw it done. That settled it, so He said, 'I am the Messiah!' There were no more questions; she went on telling everybody else, 'Come, see Who I've found'.

These three processes make us clean - a temple for his dwelling place: justification, sanctification and baptism of the Holy Ghost with Fire, that does the cleansing of this temple.

The frame of the old world was not destroyed by the waters when it was baptized in the days of Noah, only sin and the sinners that were on it. The framework remained. In II Peter the third chapter, the word world is the Greek 'kosmos' which means the 'world order' - the politics, sinners, systems, sin, disease, germs, and everything that's wrong. So justification, (as you Baptists and Methodists like to think of it), believing and being baptized, is not enough! You'll wander right back into the things of the world; cut your hair, wear shorts, and everything else. Nothing has happened yet. You just looked back and saw you'd done wrong.

What did justification do to the world? Never did a thing except wash away past sin. After the flood it started off again, with as much sin as ever there was. That's the way of a man who only goes as far as justification. Billy Graham ought to see that. He said, 'I make thirty thousand converts, and one year later, I can't find thirty'. That's because he only took them as far as justification. see? They surely repent, some of them at least. But that's not what it takes. We proved it here in the type.

So the old framework was not destroyed by the water. The world was only washed. It was baptized. And the framework will remain though it be burnt with fire. The baptism doesn't destroy the earth; it just destroys the sin that's on it.

God once shook the earth, but this time he'll shake the heavens also. For we receive a kingdom that cannot be moved, the eternal kingdom. Peter said, 'The heavens shall pass away with a great noise, and the elements shall melt with fervent heat, the earth also and the works that are therein shall be burned up'. Not the planet, the works therein: the WORKS of man.

'The heavens shall pass away with a great noise'. The whole earth will be on fire. Such an explosion has got to kill every disease, every thistle, every thorn, everything there is will be burnt up!

And it's not altogether a literal fire; it's also a holy Fire that will take away Satan and all of his demons. Both heaven and earth will pass away, killing all germs, all natural life, on and around it, even the H2O, the water, will explode. Talk about a noise!

You know, when a man receives the baptism of Fire there's a lot of noise around. They think that's a shame when people scream and shout like that. Just wait till this earth gets her baptism. The Bible said here in Revelation 21, 'And there was no more sea'. The water which is made of two gases, will explode.

This will change the surface of the entire earth! She'll burst and blow to pieces. The crust and hundreds of feet below it, will be demolished. Earth's atmosphere will ignite, and great flames will shoot lava thousands of miles into space, when it has its baptism of Fire.

'How's this world going to pass away, if we're to live on it'? The Greek word, 'pass away' does not mean, annihilation. It means to change from one CONDITION to another.

When a man's regenerated, he's been CHANGED from a sinner to a saint, not completely annihilated. He's been changed from what he WAS to what he IS.

We read in Revelation 6:14 'The heaven departed as a scroll'. Jesus said, 'heavens and earth shall pass away', or be changed. They were not annihilated, for later in revelation 21:2-24 John saw the new Jerusalem coming down from God out of heaven and sit upon THIS earth. And 'the kings of the earth will bring their glory and honor into it'. The new Jerusalem sits upon this earth, which Jesus said, 'The meek shall inherit'. It is just changed.

Daniel saw the SAME thing. When the Rock hewn without hands struck the world, the image of its systems, the ten confederated states ruling the NWO of was broken, and became like chaff on a summer threshing floor, and the WIND blew it away. Then the ROCK grew into a great MOUNTAIN that covered the earth.

You're the same person in stature that you were when God called you, it was a regeneration: the old life, and old desires, passed away. You used to like to drink, and curse, and fuss, and stew and run around, and be immoral... that thing just died. You were Satan's instrument, now you are redeemed. And the world will be redeemed the same way. A new heavens and new earth just like you are a new creature. A new creation in the SAME old temple!

And it isn't going to be another earth; it will be the same earth. The baptism of Fire only is to cleanse and make it a fit place for his meek to live in. Like he gave us the baptism of Fire before he could come and live in us. When you get that baptism of fire, it burns everything contrary to the Word out of you.

That's what we were talking last week, the evidence of the Holy Ghost. The evidence of the Holy Ghost is when you can receive the Word, not some SYSTEM, but have a clear understanding. How do you know your understanding is correct? The word will vindicate itself from Genesis to Revelation. It's got to match the entire word! To be the Bride, you have to be part of him. See? He IS the Word. And WHAT part of Him must you be? The Word that's promised for THIS day, when he's calling his Bride. You're that part. Do you get it?

He makes this earth a fit place to live through eternity. Notice, the millennium reign, this thousand years, is not the new earth. See? The millennium reign is a different reign. It's just a rest period. For in the millennium we have things that could not go into eternity. It's a type of the old seventh day in Eden, after he made the world. The seventh day in Eden, he rested.

Man has been on earth for almost six thousand years, and every two thousand years it's had a destruction. The FIRST two thousand: the flood came, and He baptized it with water. The NEXT two thousand: Jesus came to sanctify and claim it, drip His blood upon it, and call it His.

Jesus said, 'I go away to prepare a place for you, and I will come again' as King with My Queen, after the THIRD two thousand years, for the millennium. The Royal honeymoon. Then comes the white throne judgment. We're still in time in the millennium. It's one day of a thousand years, a TIME element. Don't confuse it with the new earth. Then he burns it off and regenerates it for his own perfect world, and puts his own back upon it.

TWO, plus TWO, plus TWO equals SIX days, SIX thousand years. We're right AT the Millennium, the SEVENTH day NOW. What are we waiting for? Only the earthquake marking the end of the Gentile dispensation, calling a resurrection and the manifestation of the Sons of God.

Now notice what Peter said:

1. **Repent {acknowledge and be sorry} for your sin of unbelief.**
2. **Be Baptized (by immersion in water), in the NAME of Jesus Christ.**
3. **Receive the Gift of the Holy Ghost which makes us new creatures in Christ. By faith we repent, believing in our hearts that God**

hears and forgives. By faith we are baptized in water, in the Name of the Lord Jesus Christ, testifying before many witnesses that we believe and identify with the death, burial and resurrection of our Lord Jesus. If God recognizes our faith to be genuine, from the heart, He takes the third step and gives us the Holy Ghost, sealing us into His Kingdom. Oh praise the Lord for His Grace toward us!

GRACE is "unmerited favor or treatment" and does not sweep sin under the carpet of compromising complacency. Even in the face of weakness in our flesh, by Grace we should acknowledge the righteousness of God's Word. G**race** drew us to the plan of Salvation; **Grace** provided us the Savior in the Person of our Lord Jesus. **Grace** produced the preaching of the Word to draw us unto Christ, convicting us of our need for the Savior, and **by Grace {through faith}** it is revealed to us in the Word what we must do to «enter» and become partakers of the Salvation which Jesus Christ purchased for us with His own blood. **And by faith** we repent, believing in our hearts that God hears and forgives. Salvation is a free gift, offered by Grace (the unmerited favor of God) to those who WANT it. But with it comes responsibilities.

But how come that these people just carry on and saying "**Oh, I believe** in God; He does not judge us from the outwards appearance. Or **they say oh, God knows how I believe in my heart.** And they will just dance around with their wrong and with repetitive speaking in tongues bla,bla,bla which are never interpreted and just carrying on and quoting quotes saying, **"For whoso shall call upon the name of the Lord shall be saved": They will be quick enough to say 'don't judge'. I am just as good as the other fellow". But** not all Israel are Israel. Not as though the word of God hath taken no effect. For they are not all Israel, which are of Israel: Neither, because they are the seed of Abraham, are they all children: but, In Isaac shall thy seed be called. Rom9:6-7

Watching the current trend in modern Christianity, you can agree that the religious people of the world are just more content with a "*form of godliness*" but denying to live by the **"whole" Word of God and shall heap to themselves, teachers having itching ears**. For that has NOTHING to do with your Salvation - because Salvation is a free gift with a "personal" experience between YOU and GOD. That means God doing it, and you hearing, recognizing, receiving and responding to what God has done as recorded in His Word. It is not what you think, or how sincere you want to be and be sincerely wrong; it is not your emotions or feelings but you, coming to terms in agreement with the word of God regardless. If God says it, that settles it.

"He that is of God heareth God's words:" (Jhn 8:47). Oh hallelujah, I feel like shouting and speaking in tongue right now. I feel hearing within me someone singing "I feel a change in my life. I feel the spirit right down inside my soul, I serve the God who is very much alive, I feel a change in my life". Amen! Jesus paid it all, all to Him I owe. Sins have left a crimson stain, He washed it white than snow! Glorious amen!

Come unto me all ye that are heavy laden, I will give you rest. Christian rests. It a Christian it is all over. It is all finished for the believer at Calvary. Oh, sickness may come and disappointments too; but the Christian is at rest knowing, that God is able to keep that which He has promised, and regardless of what the thing is, or how it looks, *there's neither sickness, sorrow, death, starvation or anything that can separate us from the love of God that is in Christ Jesus.* **We are at rest!** Take my yoke upon you, and learn of me; for I am meek and lowly. Matt 11:28-29.

As the song writer sang his song: the anchor holds, though the ship has been badly battered, though the sails are torn, the anchor holds. **Now some people think, "Because they go and join a church, and put their names on the book, that's all they have to do." While other people think, "because they shout, and that's all they have to do." Great majority of the people also believing, "because they speak with tongues, oh that is all they have to do." Of course some think, "Because they got power to heal the sick, and that is all they have to do." No sir! It is not so. It is the grace of God that saves you, God's amazing grace.**

Apostle Paul said, in 1 Corinthians 13, "Though I speak with tongue of men and Angels, though I have discernment, though I have gifts, to feed the poor, though I can move mountains with faith, though I have knowledge to understand all things, I am nothing till love comes in, which is grace." God has to do it. You can do all these things and still be lost. Oh it is grace, God's grace to the human race.

Paul wrote Abraham's commentary, he never mentioned one thing about Abraham's unbelief, never was it even accounted to him. "Abraham staggered not at the promise of God through unbelief, but was strong, giving praise to God" *My humble prayer is, for God to look at me through His blood by his grace and that He won't see my mistakes. Oh Grant it Lord!*

SALVA|ION

WHAT IS SALVATION AND WHY DO WE NEED SALVATION?

*I*n the Bible, the word "**Salvation**" implies "**deliverance**" or "**Victory**" - to be **delivered (saved) from**, or gain the **victory over the influence** of something or someone in our lives which causes us to act contrary to the Word and Will of God. To answer the Questions of **WHAT** is Salvation and **WHY** do we need it we have to go back to the beginning to a time when man didn't need to be delivered from, or get the victory over anything.

In the beginning, in God's perfect creation, in the Garden of Eden, all was positive, **all nature was in perfect harmony with God's will**. And as long as our first parents (Adam and Eve) lived in perfect harmony with God and with His Will for their lives, they had no need of Salvation. In fact, while living in the Garden, in God's perfect environment they had no knowledge of what would later be known as **"God's Plan Of Salvation"**. **But, the peace, rest and joy of that perfect world was shattered when "ONE" Word of God was broken (disobeyed)**.

The Bible tells us in ***Genesis 1:31, "And God saw every thing that he had made, and, behold, (it was) very good."*** Then in **Genesis 2:9** we find that God "planted" a special Garden, called Eden, and man would live in this garden - it was a utopia and would have remained thus as long as the man and his wife **"chose"** to **"obey"** God. When God "formed" man out of the dust of the earth He made him a **"free moral agent"** with the **"power to choose"** what **to do** and **not to do** - obey or disobey. **But up to this point in God's creation man had only the knowledge of God - there was nothing to choose between;** therefore, he just worshipped and obeyed God. But God would **"test"** the **"power of choice"** he had given His son and daughter.

In Genesis 2:9..., we're told, "And out of the ground made the LORD God to grow every tree that is pleasant to the sight, and good for food; the tree of life also in the midst of the garden, and the tree of knowledge of good and evil." The first Tree is clearly identified - the Tree of LIFE (Jesus Christ); the second tree is referred to as containing the "knowledge of good AND evil" (The Devil). When man was placed in the garden the Lord specifically warned him about this tree, saying, "...Of every tree of the garden thou mayest freely eat: But of the tree of the knowledge of good and evil, thou shalt not eat of it: for in the day that thou eatest thereof thou shalt surely die". In no uncertain terms man was told that partaking of what the Tree of Knowledge of Good and Evil offered would surely end in death.

In Deuteronomy 30:19 God warned Israel, saying, "I call heaven and earth to record this day against you, [that] I have set before you life and death, blessing and cursing: therefore choose life, that both thou and thy seed may live:" It applied to Adam and Eve; it applied to Israel and it applies to all of us. Everyday we're confronted with the choice to partake of the Tree of Life (by obedience to God's Word) or partake of the tree of knowledge of good and evil (by disobedience).

In the Garden of Eden God gave Adam and Eve only "**one command**" to choose to keep; and in **Genesis 3** we find that **Eve was deceived** into partaking of the "*tree of knowledge of good and evil*" (the Serpent). She allowed the Devil to "change only ONE word" of what God had said. God said, *"thou shalt surely die"*. The Serpent said *shall NOT surely die"*. Eve stopped long enough to allow the Devil to get her to "reason" on the Word of God.

Referring back to this the Apostle Paul in 2nd. Corinthians 11:13 warned the early church with these words, "But I fear, lest by any means, as the serpent beguiled Eve through his subtilty, so your minds should be corrupted from the simplicity that is in Christ."

But the deed was done - **"Eve chose" to believe the Devil's lies and reasoning**. Sharing her newfound **carnal knowledge** with Adam, **he chose** to partake with her, to identify with her sin, trusting that God would, in redeeming and giving Salvation to him, would also redeem and give Salvation to his wife. **By the GRACE**

of God, this is what our Lord Jesus did - He **(through Grace)** put Himself in the likeness of sinful flesh with us, died [shedding innocent Blood to atone for our sins] and rose again, to redeem and give Salvation to Adam's fallen sons and daughters and bring us BACK to Himself again.

Let's just drop this thought in right here: **God "permitted" sin** to raise it's ugly head. He never caused it, but by His "permissive" will, He "permitted" Adam and Eve to do what they did. **Satan's interference would be God's opportunity to reveal all of His Divine attributes to His children**. NOW, His children would see HIS glorious attributes in full manifestation - Agapo Love, Savior, Father, Son, Holy Spirit, Healer, Judge, Eternal Life, Resurrection, etc.; **and seeing these attributes we would love him for Himself**.

Our first parents **chose to disobey** God's plain command "not to partake of the tree of knowledge of good and evil". Their choice plunged the whole world in sin and death. Now began the great battle of the ages - between God and Satan - the battle for the minds of men and women. **NOW, Man [all the human race] was in dire need of salvation** - deliverance from and victory over the influence of Satan and sin in his/her life. **Man and woman by their own choosing** became subject to sin and death. Today, by our own choosing we can obtain Salvation and deliverance from sin and death, and one day enter into a new heaven and a new earth where sin and death will be forever conquered.

But, in the beginning, **because of a wrong choice** man was driven out of the Paradise of God. Physically, he was now under the curse - *"**dust thou art and unto dust shalt thou return**"*. But **man was given hope** in **the promise** of **Genesis 3:15** which spoke of the coming of a Redeemer to pay the price for man's sin and give him Salvation and Victory over the world, the flesh and the Devil.

Every messenger of God would now point to that promise of Salvation. Before the Crucifixion drama all Divine Revelation from God pointed **forward** to that day when Messiah would come and redeem man; but for the last 2000 years every messenger and Divine Revelation from God has been pointing **back** to Calvary. **Salvation, not for the Devil's children, but for all God's children, would be according to their faith in What Christ would accomplish for them in His death, burial and resurrection.** Every Messenger is charged with the responsibility of leading the true sons and daughters of God in the way of true Salvation, as opposed to Satan, through his messengers leading millions down the path of false religion and the end thereof are the ways of death **(Proverbs 14:12)**.

In working out (by Grace) our own Salvation with fear and trembling **(Philippians 2:12)** before God we must **remember** that the *"**tree of knowledge of good AND evil**"* is **still in the garden of God**, tempting us to "**add to**" or "**take away**" from the whole Word of the Lord. As we continue in our study of the subject of Salvation, keep in mind that *"**Man shall not live by bread alone, but by EVERY WORD that proceedeth out of the mouth of God" (Matthew 4:4).***

grace and SALVATION!

On this subject, I would like to reiterate what I said earlier for clarity sake. Now, one of the most misunderstood doctrines of the Bible is "**Salvation by Grace through faith**", which now has been warped with the modern-day teaching of "Grace" that it now looks like nothing but disgraceful and reproach to Christianity.

What the Grace actually reveals in God's Bible as Sin, worldliness, abominations and iniquity, that many of these modern-day preachers now for the fear of losing their members are so afraid to preach against sin, and so hide under the "guise" of Grace, thereby making a disgrace out of the grace of God to mankind. How can? Rather than speak against sin, they engage themselves more on signs and miracles, and **money seed sowing, when Jesus already said that the seed sown was the word of God. Luke 8:5-15.**

⁵A sower went out to sow his seed: and as he sowed, some fell by the wayside; and it was trodden down, and the fowls of the air devoured it.

⁶ And some fell upon a rock; and as soon as it was sprung up, it withered away, because it lacked moisture.

⁷ And some fell among thorns; and the thorns sprang up with it, and choked it.

⁸ And other fell on good ground, and sprang up, and bare fruit an hundredfold. And when he had said these things, he cried, He that hath ears to hear, let him hear.

⁹ And his disciples asked him, saying, What might this parable be?

¹⁰ And he said, Unto you it is given to know the mysteries of the kingdom of God: but to others in parables; that seeing they might not see, and hearing they might not understand.

NOW THE PARABLE IS THIS: The seed is the word of God; IT IS THE WORD AND NOT MONEY!

According to Jhn 3:7, **marvel not that I said unto thee**, ye must be BORN AGAIN! And when you are BORN AGAIN, it is not because you believe. They say, you are born when you believe. But the Bible said that the **Devil believes, also.** Now, notice, it is not that, it is an experience. You say, Well, I have lived a good life. So did the apostles also, **but they were not BORN AGAIN until they received the Holy Spirit. They were not even converted until they had received the Holy Spirit.** You remember the night, just before the betrayal took place? **Jesus said to Simon Peter, when thou art converted, then strengthen thy brethren.** And Peter had followed Him for three and a half years, and had cast out devils, and healed the sick, had preached the Gospel, and still according to the Word was not yet even converted.

No matter how good we are, how much we go to church, or do this, we got to be BORN AGAIN. See? It must be. And God told Adam what he could do and what he could not do. He placed him behind His Word. And then the enemy come in, by deceit, and crawled through the walls of God's Word, cause the door was open to him, and he marred that image, to sin. That's one of the saddest stories."

¹² Those by the way side are they that hear; **then cometh the devil, and taketh away the "word" out of their hearts**, lest they should believe and be saved.

¹³ They on the rock are they, which, when **they hear, receive the word** with joy; and these have no root, which for a while believe, and in time of temptation fall away.

¹⁴ And that which fell among thorns are they, which, when they have heard, go forth, and are choked with cares and riches and pleasures of this life, and bring no fruit to perfection.

¹⁵ But that on the good ground are they, which in an honest and good **heart, having heard the word**, keep it, and bring forth fruit with patience.

But the scriptures say seek ye first the kingdom of God and his righteousness and all other things shall be added unto thee.

Howbeit, Isaiah 58:1 said, "Cry aloud, spare not, lift up thy voice like a trumpet, and shew my people their transgression, and the house of Jacob their sins." **This is what God by His "Grace" does - HE REVEALS OUR LOST CONDITION AND SHOWS US THE WAY TO SALVATION.** Grace DOES NOT sweep sin under the carpet of compromising due to complacency. Shall we continue in sin, that grace may abound? God forbids! Rom 6:1. Even in the face of weakness in our flesh, by Grace we will acknowledge the rightness of God's Word.

If we truly have a relationship with God, from the beginning to the end it is ALL based-on GRACE, the unmerited favor of a Loving God. The great plan of

Salvation finds its root in the GRACE of God. When man, because of his sin in the Garden of Eden, fell from favor with God, then Divine Love projected, Divine Grace provided the Promise of a Redeemer in Genesis 3:15.

It was Grace before the Law; Grace during the Law because man without the indwelling Holy Spirit could not keep the Law. It's Grace after the Law: and Grace gave the promise, Grace sent prophets and Messengers to keep us in line with the Word; and Grace sent our Messiah - Redeemer to pay the price for our sin and restore true fellowship with the Father again. Oh hallelujah, amen!

But now we found out that, when expounding the "Way of Salvation" most people OUT OF CONTEXT, refer to Ephesians 2:8, and then leaving men and women in their congregation, with the wrong **impression that being "saved by Grace" consists of 'accepting Jesus as their Savior, thereby giving Him "lip-service" once in a while, and continue living the same kind of lives they always lived in the past. Absolutely wrong and heretic!**

The truth is that, in reality "Grace leads to a Salvation wherein Christ is the LORD" of the individual's life (Luke 6:46); and the individual becomes a "new creation in Christ, with a new spiritual nature which seeks daily to please the Lord Jesus Christ, asking for a daily measure of Grace to stay in line with **the Word." 2 Corinthians 5:17.**

Let us consider ALL what Ephesians 2:8 says: **For by grace are ye saved through faith; and that not of yourselves: it is the gift of God:** Many people quote only this first part of the verse: "By grace are ye save..."; but the full text says, "By Grace are ye save THROUGH faith".

Therefore, Salvation is "BY Grace THROUGH Faith" The channel through which Grace operates is "Faith". Grace does nothing for us and can do nothing for us unless there is "Faith" there to receive AND believe what Grace offers.

Therefore, God gives us the "Faith" to receive the gift of Salvation which Grace offers. We do not deserve it but God, through His unmerited favor offers it to us. Paul, in Hebrews 11:6 shows how important faith is in our relationship with God: "But without faith it is impossible to please him: for he that cometh to God must believe that he is, and that he is a rewarder of them that diligently seek him".

On the Day of Pentecost, in Acts 2:37-38, we see "By GRACE through Faith" in action. God by His grace had drawn all these people together to hear the preaching of the Word that would give them the Faith (revelation) of Salvation. Peter preached onto the people the Revelation of Jesus Christ, expounding unto them the things that God was doing in their day and what God had accomplished in the death and resurrection of Jesus of Nazareth. And as always, the preaching of the Word convicted the heart and conscience of the predestined sons and daughters of God. The Bible clearly says:

"Now when they heard this, they were pricked {convicted} in their heart, and said unto Peter and to the rest of the apostles, men, and brethren, what shall we do?

That is the question we all need to find the answer to: "What shall we DO to be saved?" Let us take note of Peter's answer:

"Then Peter said unto them, Repent, and be baptized every one of you in the name of Jesus Christ for the remission of sins, and ye shall receive the gift of the Holy Ghost. For the promise is unto you [Jews], and to your children [Jews], and to all that are afar off [Gentiles], even as many as the Lord our God shall call [Jews and Gentiles]."

Peter was VERY SPECIFIC in his answer. He left no room for doubt or any more questions. Now, we see "FAITH" coming into play. By Grace [through faith] God reveals what He required of them and what He requires of us that we may enter into His Salvation - it is a "test" of the sincerity of our desire for Salvation - how far are we willing to go in our obedience to the Lord?

Peter said:

1. Repent {acknowledge and be sorry} for their sin and unbelief.
2. Be Baptized (by immersion in water), in the NAME of Jesus Christ.
3. Receive the Gift of the Holy Ghost which makes us new creatures in Christ.

Grace provides the instructions, but it is left to us to obey. By faith we repent, believing in our hearts that God hears and forgives. By faith we are baptized in water in the Name of the Lord Jesus Christ, testifying before witnesses that we believe in and identify with the death, burial, and resurrection of our Lord Jesus. If God recognizes our faith to be genuine, from the heart, He takes the third step and gives us the Holy Ghost, sealing us into His Kingdom. Praise the Lord for His Grace toward us!

Grace drew up the plan of Salvation; Grace provided a Savior in the Person of our Lord Jesus Christ; Grace produced the preaching of the Word to draw us unto Christ, convicting us of our need of that Savior, and by Grace {through faith} it's revealed to us in the Word what we must do to "enter into" and become a partaker of the Salvation which Jesus Christ purchased for us with His own blood.

In plain and simple language, GRACE is "unmerited favor or treatment". Being born in sin and shaped in iniquity (Psalm 51), walking, and living contrary to the Word and nature of God, we did not deserve Salvation. **But God, by His grace provided a plan to save as many of those of His seed that are ordained and predestinated to be saved all over the world.**

Then Grace THROUGH Faith 'reveals' the plan to our hearts and believing it, we walk in obedience to what is revealed to us. Heb 10:29 tells us that some [taking God's Word lightly] are guilty of insulting the spirit of Grace. It is important that we respect ALL of God's Word for it is "the goodness (grace) of God leadeth thee to repentance". (Rom 2:4).

Now we can see that Salvation is a daily living life-changing experience between the repentant sinner and God. Beginning in time, and it climaxes in eternity. It's an experience that comes to the believer in three distinct steps or phases. (1) JUSTIFICATION; (2) SANCTIFICATION and (3) The BAPTISM OF THE

HOLY GHOST (the new birth). Every born-again believer will experience this in his/her life.

You Are Completely Saved and Can Never Lose Your Salvation! But If You Lose the Joy of Your Salvation, It Can Be Restored! If You Are Truly Saved, And Not a Reprobate.

Fallen from grace? That certainly sounds like they have never lost their salvation!

Restore unto me the joy of thy salvation; and uphold me with thy free spirit. Psalm 51:12.

When we hear in the news about a celebrity who has "fallen from grace", it typically describes someone who was behaving well but then suffered a moral decadence or a moral failure. Perhaps they were arrested for illegal drugs, cheated on their spouse, or cheated on their taxes. David cried to the Lord one time, "Lord, restore to me the joy of my salvation. You are still a Christian, but you need to turn loose of everything that you know how, and seek God, and pray.

But in Galatians, falling from grace means something very different: falling away from the message of God's grace and toward the Law. Paul wrote Galatians to a variety of people. Some had accepted the Gospel; others were acquainted with the message but had not accepted it. Still others had flirted with the idea of salvation by grace through faith but instead chose to seek rightness with God through keeping the Law.

You are either saved or you are not saved. You are a saint or a sinner, one or the other, and your spiritual attitude towards God's Word identifies you exactly where you are standing. Some of our most frequent spiritual questions relate to the loss of salvation: But what if I die by suicide? But what if I get a divorce and then remarry? But what if I commit the same sin, willfully, over and over again?

These four words pester us: But what if I . . .? However, God already saw our concerns coming. He dealt with them entirely through the new covenant by anchoring us to a promise that He made to Himself.

We don't maintain or sustain any part of God's promise to Himself. As believers who are forever in Christ, the "But what if I . . .?" questions do not have to plague us. We are not even in the equation!

And remember, when the Lamb was slain, your salvation was included in the Sacrifice, because the Bible said that your name was written on the Lamb's Book of Life before the foundation of the world. What about that? Then what are we going to do? It is God that showeth mercy. It is God that called you. It is God that chose you in Christ before the foundation of the world. Jesus said, "You never chose Me; I chose you. And I knew you before the foundation of the world."

Instead of asking, "But what if I . . .?" we need to be asking, "But what if God . . .?" And the answer to that question is a resounding yes: God did the very thing He needed to do to secure us forever. He promised Himself that He would never leave us: If we are faithless, He remains faithful, for He cannot deny Himself. 2Tim 2:13. God placed His Spirit in us. He cannot contradict or disown Himself. So, He will never disown us! This was all part of God's perfect plan to secure us forever in Jesus.

And it is this security in Jesus that inspires and motivates us to live uprightly Titus 2:11-12.

If YOU HAVE FALLEN WEAK, OR BECOME LUKEWARM, IN YOUR EXPERIENCE, YOU' WOULD LIKE TO BE RENEWED AGAIN.... David said, "RESTORE TO ME THE JOY OF MY SALVATION." He had NOT LOST HIS SALVATION, but HE LOST ALL HIS JOY. I THINK that goes to ABOUT NINETY- FIVE PERCENT of THE CHURCH TODAY - LOSING THE JOY OF THEIR SALVATION. "RESTORE TO ME THE JOY OF MY SALVATION."

This prayer implies that, you can lose the joy of your salvation and can get it renewed, Hear Jesus prayers in John 17:11-12. And now I am no more in the world, but these are in the world, and I come to thee. Holy Father keep through thine own name those whom thou hast given me, that they may be one, as we are. 12 While I was with them in the world, I KEPT THEM IN THY NAME: THOSE THAT THOU HAST GAVEST ME I HAVE KEPT, AND "NONE OF THEM IS LOST" BUT THE SON OF PERDITION; that the scripture might be fulfilled. Well, you say, "now, brother Branham, I guess once in grace always in grace." That brings a lot of disgrace.

But when a man or woman has been born of the spirit of God, old things have passed away, all things have become new, and he's birthed and blessed by the Eternal God. And they can no longer perish than God himself can perish. Do you mean to tell me that the Infinite God would come down and give you Eternal Life knowing that he was going to lose you? Save you here, knowing He is going to lose you there? What then did he save you for? Why, is he going to work against himself. If he saved you once you are saved for all Eternity.

There is no demon in hell could upset make you lose it. Some think they are saved, and are not saved, but working up under emotion and think you are saved, you need faith to believe it's the grace of God upon your life. You might feel like you are saved, you might believe you are saved, you might think you are saved, you might join a church and they put down your name in their book and you deceive yourself thinking that you have been saved. You might be a good Catholic, Baptist, Methodist, or Pentecostal. That has nothing to do with it. **If you are ever saved, you were saved before the foundation of the world.**

STEPS TO SALVATION

Though very religious, **the people in this Age know very little about Salvation**. Not long ago a young man shocked his grandmother with this question: *"Nan, why do people celebrate Easter?"* That young man's parents did go to church occasionally, but what little religion they had was always left inside the church door when they went home. For most people, the extent of their religious faith is going to church (regularly or occasionally), being good to your neighbor, etc. **Compared to Bible Salvation, the Salvation offered by many churches is wishy-washy - the kind of Salvation that 'whitewashes' sin to make it appear good and acceptable.**

For many their everyday religious experience doesn't even come within a hundred miles of the "golden rule" which instructs us: *"**And as ye** would that men should, do to YOU, do ye also to THEM likewise"* (**Luke 6:31**). **They have not** been taught; **nor have they** taken the time to search the Scriptures to learn that Bible Salvation is a **constant** walk with God, **daily growing and maturing** in our relationship and **gaining** more victory over the **influence** of the World and the things of the World in our fleshly bodies.

At the beginning of our study we stated that "Salvation" implies "deliverance from [saved]" or "Victory over" the influence of something or someone in our lives which causes us to act contrary to the Word and Will of God. Many profess Salvation but one is caused to wonder WHAT they have been delivered saved from and WHAT they have victory over! They continue living the same kind of lives they always lived, with no indication of the "new creation - new nature" which the Bible speaks off. **Somewhere they have stopped short of** *"believing unto the Salvation of their souls"* (Hebrews 10:39).

They have failed to *"follow on to KNOW the Lord"* (Hosea 6:3) and heed Jesus' exhortation to *"Continue in His Word"* (John 8:31).

If they follow the Bible's "Steps to Salvation" the end result is the 'birth" of a "new you" in your soul. Jesus said in John 3:3, "Verily, verily, I say unto thee, except a man be born again, he cannot see [understand] the kingdom of God." In the 1st. Epistle of Peter 1:2223 we find more insight into the "new birth" through these Words: "Seeing ye have purified your souls in obeying the truth through the Spirit unto unfeigned love of the brethren, [see that ye] love one another with a pure heart fervently:

Being born again, not of corruptible seed, but of incorruptible, by the word of God, which liveth and abideth forever." One thing is certain - if you ever experience Salvation from the Lord, you are a "changed" person - the nature of your soul is changed, your desires are different, you feed daily on God's Word (the Bible), lining up with it's precepts, your motives and objectives in life are different and God is "number One" in your life. Many of the followers attempt to avoid facing the FULL issue of Bible Salvation by saying, "Oh, I believe in God; I am not so bad; I am just as good as the other fellow".

But that has NOTHING to do with Salvation. Salvation is a "personal" transaction between YOU and GOD - God doing it, and you hearing, recognizing, receiving, and acting on {responding to} what God has done and recorded in His Word. The Apostle said, "He that is of God heareth God's words:" (John 8:47). And what is written for one is written for all! Apostle Paul said: "But though we, or an angel from heaven, preach any other gospel unto you than that which we have preached unto you, let him be accursed" (Galatians 1:8).

Before proceeding to the discussion of **"The Steps to Salvation"** - the out-working of God's Salvation in our lives, let's read these few Scriptures which speak of Salvation... I will take the cup of salvation and call upon the name of the LORD. (Psalms 116:13). Neither is there salvation in any other: for there is none other name under heaven given among men, whereby we must be saved. (Acts 4:12)

For I am not ashamed of the gospel of Christ: for it is the power of God unto salvation to everyone that believeth; (Romans 1:16).

For godly sorrow worketh repentance to salvation. (2Cor. 7:10).

Work out your own salvation with fear and trembling. (Philippians 2:12). Salvation is a living life-changing experience between the repentant sinner and God.

Beginning from the time of your response to the call, to the time it climaxes into eternity, it's an experience that comes to the believer in three distinct steps or phases. (1) Justification; (2) Sanctification and (3) The Baptism of the Holy Ghost (the new birth). Every born- again believer experience this in his/her life. This is God's work in them.

FOR WHAT PURPOSE DID CHRIST DIE?

Apostle Paul said that Christ died for all the people, even the non-elect, and many times I have heard people say, 'Yes, Christ died for all people but not all people in the same way.'

However, I am having adequate trouble going to explain how for what tangible reason Christ died for the non-elect.

BOTH-AND SAVIOR

Let's start with 1 Timothy 4:10, which captures the both-and. It goes like this, "For to this end we toil and strive, because we have our hope set on the living God, who is the Savior of all people, especially of those who believe." Notice the phrase "the Savior of all, especially of those who believe."

"For the elect, the blood of Jesus is the blood of the new covenant, which purchases for them a new heart."

Paul says in Titus 2:11, "For the grace of God has appeared, bringing salvation for all people." And Paul would add, "especially those who believe": "He brought salvation for all, especially for those who believe."

We can see the both-and in the gospel of John. Start with John 3:16: "For God so loved the world, that he gave his only Son, that whoever believes in him should not perish but have eternal life." Christ came as an expression of God's love for the world. Then John says, "For God did not send his Son into the world to condemn the world, but in order that the world might be saved through him" (John 3:17). The offering of his Son is the offering of salvation to the world.

NOW, THE QUESTION IS FOR WHAT TANGIBLE REASON DID CHRIST die for?

Electing Love

First, we need to see the other side of the coin in the Gospel of John, besides saving the whole world.

"I am the good shepherd. I know my own and my own know me, just as the Father knows me and I know the Father; and I lay down my life for the sheep. And I have other sheep that are not of this fold. I must bring them also, and they will listen to my voice. So there will be one flock, one shepherd. For this reason the Father loves me, because I lay down my life that I may take it up again." (John 10:14–17)

"I am the good shepherd. I know my own and my own know me, just as the Father knows me and I know the Father; and I lay down my life for the sheep" — the ones who know me, the ones that the Father's given me. "And I have other sheep that are not of this fold" those are the elect scattered throughout the world. "I must bring them also. They will listen to my voice" - that's what marks them out as sheep (John 10:14-16).

In other words, Jesus said, "I go out. I preach. I call. The sheep, the ones whom the Father has, he gives to me. They recognize my voice. They come to me. There will be one flock and one shepherd" (John 10:16). The Father has the sheep. He gives the sheep to Jesus. They are his own. They know his voice. He calls them. They come. He lays down his life for them - uniquely for them (John 10:17–18).

Paul says the same thing in Ephesians 5:25: "Husbands, love your wives, as Christ loved the church and gave himself up for her." The husband loves his wife uniquely and in a special way. That's the way Christ loves the church and dies for the church — in a unique way.

THE GREATEST GIFT

Now, what's the effect of this focused, particular redemption for the bride, the sheep, the elect? What does the death do that's unique for the bride? I think Romans 8:32 gives the answer: "He who did not spare his own Son, but gave him up for us all" now pause. "Christ accomplished a completely full and satisfactory and effective redemption for whoever believes."

The "us all" in the context of Romans 8:32 is clearly the elect. It's not the whole world. It's the elect. "He did not spare his own Son, but gave him up for us all." You can see this in the next verse: "Who shall bring any charge against God's elect? It is God who justifies. Who is to condemn?" (Romans 8:33–34). That's how verse 32 is being fulfilled, and you can see it in the rest of this verse.

"He who did not spare his own Son but gave him up for us all, how will he not also with him graciously give us all things?" In other words, the death of Christ for his people secures and guarantees for them every saving blessing there is.

"Will he not also with him graciously give us all things?" Yes, he will because that is what the death of Christ guarantees for all the elect. If God gave his Son in this same way for every person on the planet, then that promise would attach to every person because it's attached to the blood of Jesus, to the sacrifice of Jesus. That means every person would be saved, would be guaranteed every possible blessing, which Paul says clearly is not the case (in places like 2 Thessalonians 1:9).

NOT AN OFFER

What can we say about how the death of Christ expresses itself for the elect and the non-elect who reject him? How is it different? For the elect, the blood of Jesus is the blood of the new covenant, which purchases for them, a new heart, new life, faith, and obedience.

Jesus says that in Luke 22:20: "This cup that is poured out for you is the new covenant in my blood." The blood of Jesus is purchasing the new covenant.

The new covenant is not an offer of salvation. It's an accomplishment of salvation in the hearts of God's people.

He gives them a new heart and a new spirit, a gift of life, gift of faith, gift of obedience.

ALL CAN COME

Now, back to John 3:16 for the other side of how the death of Christ relates to the world, or to the non-elect. I think the wording of John 3:16 provides the answer of how to speak of the gift of Christ, the death of Christ, for the non-elect, the whole world.

"You may look everyone in the eye and say, 'Believe on the Lord Jesus Christ, and you will never perish.'"

Here's how he puts it: "God so loved the world, that he gave his only Son, that whoever believes in him should not perish but have eternal life." He loved the world so that everyone who believes would have life.

The way to speak about the giving of the Son as an expression of love to the world is to highlight the word that: "That whoever believes in him should not perish but have eternal life."

That's the connection we make between the death of Christ and every person on this planet. Christ accomplished a completely full and satisfactory and effective redemption for whosoever believes.

You may look (and should look) everyone in the eye absolutely everyone in your neighborhood, at your church, at your work — and say, "Believe on the Lord Jesus Christ, and you will never perish. Believe on him, and you will become a full and complete participant in the perfect salvation, the perfect payment for sins, the perfect propitiation of the wrath of God, the perfect obedience for imputation, the perfect deliverance from death and hell and Satan and into the everlasting glory of God. All of that is yours it's yours for the believing because of Jesus's death."

We could never talk like that to people — we don't know who the non-elect are so let's just assume there's lots of them that are listening — if Jesus hadn't died the way he did. That is a great and awesome gift that we are indebted to give to the entire world. Oh, that God would put fire in our hearts to take that message to the ends of the earth.

THE TRUE WATER BAPTISM

I have thought it very wise to include this topic here. For the purpose of the subject of this book, Salvation by Grace Through Faith, it is necessary to discuss about the True Water Baptism for the new beginners in Christ and those who would like to know the truth about the gospel of our Lord Jesus Christ.

If you have truly repented, and **believed on the Lord Jesus Christ**, you are supposed to be baptized immediately.

Acts 10:47

Can any man forbid water, that these should not be baptized, which have received the Holy Ghost as well as we?

This action brings you into fellowship of the believers.

We believe that by water baptism we are brought into fellowship.

But by the baptism of the Holy Spirit, we are brought into membership with Christ, of the body of Christ which is all over the world.

Now, the first time baptism was ever spoken about, was by John the Baptist. Matt 3:1, Mk 1:4. And John baptized the people in the river of Jordan, commanding them that they should repent, and get right with God, and sell their goods, and feed the poor, and the soldiers be satisfied with their money, and to get right with God.

And he baptized them in the river of Jordan, not sprinkled them, not poured them, but immersed them. The second time baptism was ever spoke of Jesus commissioned it, Matthew 28:19.

¹⁹ Go ye therefore, and teach all nations, baptizing them in the name of the Father, and of the Son, and of the Holy Ghost: The third time baptism was spoke of was Acts 2:38. Then Peter said unto them, **Repent, and be baptized** every one of you **in the name of Jesus Christ** for the remission of sins, and ye shall receive the gift of the Holy Ghost.

The next time baptism was spoken of was in the Acts 8:12. But when they believed Philip preaching the things concerning the kingdom of God, and **in the name of Jesus Christ, they were baptized, both men and women.** Acts 16. The next time baptism was spoken of was in Acts10:48.

Aquila and Priscilla in Acts18 had visited Apollo they were Baptists. And Paul went to them, and he said, "Have ye received the Holy Ghost since you have believed?" And they said, "We know not whether there be any Holy Ghost." He said, "How was you baptized?" I know in the King James it says, "unto what"; in the original, it said "unto how."

"What or how were you baptized?"

They said, "We have been baptized by the same man that baptized Jesus, John." Paul said, "That won't work no more. You got to be baptized over again." And when they heard this, they come back into the water and were rebaptized **in the Name of Jesus Christ.** Paul laid his hands upon them, and the Holy Ghost came on them. Now, if that-if Father, Son, and Holy Ghost, says here, and the Lord Jesus Christ, says here, I can't hit both targets. It has got to be right.

Jesus commanded them to baptize in a Name, not in a title. "Father, Son, and Holy Ghost" are titles.

For example: are you a son or daughter? Is your name "Son" or "Daughter?" Your parents might call you "son" or "daughter," but you have a name, and so does God. The answer is simple: Jesus Christ is God, and He is not three separate deities. He is One. Thus, the Scripture says, "One Lord, one faith, one baptism," (Eph 4:5), and

"For there are three that bear record in heaven, the Father, the Word, and the Holy Ghost: and **these three are one."** (I John 5:7)

Does it really matter that we are baptized according to what the Bible teaches? Or does any baptism work?

It mattered so much to the apostles that they re-baptized those who were not baptized correctly, even those who were baptized by the greatest of all the prophets: John the Baptist.

Soon after he received the Holy Ghost in the upper room, Peter preached a sermon about the Deity of the Lord Jesus. The people were so moved by his sermon that they asked, "What shall we do?" Peter, now filled with the Holy Ghost, answered, "Repent, and be baptized every one of you **in the name of Jesus Christ** for the remission of sins, and ye shall receive the gift of the Holy Ghost. For the promise is unto you, and to your children, and to all that are afar off, even as many as the Lord our God shall call." (Acts 2:14-39)

And with those words, we see the formula for receiving the same Holy Ghost that Peter and the apostles had at the day of Pentecost.

The Book of Acts (Chapter 19) gives us another, very clear, example of this formula in action when Paul came to a group of people in Ephesus who had already accepted Jesus as their Savior. They told him of their conversion, and he asked, "Have ye received the Holy Ghost since ye believed?" They knew Jesus, but they did not know about the Holy Ghost. Paul, knowing the right formula, asked, "Unto what then were ye baptized?" They responded that they had been baptized in a different way, according to the way John the Baptist baptized. Paul then commanded them to be baptized again, this time in the Name of the Lord Jesus. What happened next? You guessed it; they were filled with the Holy Ghost.

So, the burning question should be:

If I have been baptized in the titles of the Father, Son, and Holy Ghost, then do I need to be baptized over again?

The Book of Acts says you do. After that, you have the Promise that you WILL receive the Holy Ghost.

Who can baptize:

That is why you come here, that is why you come to Christ, you are feeding on His Word. And if you can have a time like this, here, just by His expressed attributes, what will it be when we come into His Presence? Oh, it will be wonderful! **Each one of you has the right to heal the sick, lay your hands upon the sick. Each one of you has the right to baptize.**

Matthew 3:16 And Jesus, when he was baptized, went up straightway out **of the water**: and, lo, the heavens were opened unto him, and he saw the Spirit of God descending like a dove, and lighting upon him: Mark 1: I indeed have baptized you **with water**: but he shall baptize you with the Holy Ghost. John 3:23

And John also was baptizing in Aenon near to Salim because **there was much water there:** and thy came and were baptized.

Matthew 28:18-2.

[18] And Jesus came and spake unto them, saying, all power is given **unto me in heaven and in earth.**

[19] Go ye therefore, and teach all nations, baptizing them in the name of the Father, and of the Son, and of the Holy Ghost:

[20] Teaching them to observe all things whatsoever I have commanded you: and, lo, I am with you always, even unto the end of the world. Amen

[38] Then Peter said unto them, Repent, and **be baptized every one of** you **in the name of Jesus Christ** for the remission of sins, and ye shall receive the gift of the Holy Ghost.

[39] For the promise is unto you, and to your children, and to all that are afar off, even as many as the Lord our God shall call

Acts 4:12. Neither is there salvation in any other: **for there is none other name** under heaven given among men, whereby we must be saved. Acts 8:12. But when they believed Philip preaching the things concerning the kingdom of God, and **the name of Jesus Christ,** they were baptized, both men and women.

Acts 8:36-38

[36] And as they went on their way, they came unto a certain water: and the eunuch said, See, **here is water**; what doth hinder me to be baptized?

[37] And Philip said, If thou believest with all thine heart, thou mayest. And he answered and said, I believe that Jesus Christ is the Son of God.

[38] And he commanded the chariot to stand still: and they went down both **into the water**, both Philip and the eunuch; and he baptized him.

[Note that Philip was a deacon, and he baptized the eunuch. Brother Branham said, "Each one of you has the right to baptize."

Acts 19:3-6. 3 And he said unto them, unto what then were ye baptized?

And they said, Unto John's baptism.

[4] Then said Paul, John verily baptized with the baptism of repentance, saying unto the people, that they should believe on him which should come after him, that is, on Christ Jesus.

⁵ When they heard this, they were baptized in the name of the Lord Jesus.

⁶ And when Paul had laid his hands upon them, the Holy Ghost came on them; and they spoke with tongues and prophesied.

Ephesians 4:5. One Lord, one faith, **one baptism**, I John 5:7

For there are three that bear record in heaven, the Father, the Word, and the Spirit.

For more clarity purposes, we wish to lay additional emphasis on this topic of the TRUE WATER BAPTISM as a basic fundamental requirement to a Christian's salvation!

THE TRUTH ON
WATER BAPTISM

{PART 2} BY PASTOR ZOE DEMBE

MARK 16:16 states, "He that believeth and is baptized shall be SAVED; but he that believeth NOT shall be damned."

I Peter 3:21 also reads, "The like figure whereunto {even} baptism doth also now SAVE us {not the putting away of the filth of the flesh, but the answer of a good conscience toward God}, by the resurrection of Jesus Christ."

A SERIES OF QUESTIONS USUALLY ARISE IN WATER BAPTISM: "WHAT IS THE TRUE BIBLICAL WAY OF WATER BAPTISM?" Is baptism performed by sprinkling? Or is it by immersion in water? Is it using the TITLES of Father, Son and Holy Ghost (Matt. 28:19), or using the NAME of the Lord Jesus Christ? {Acts 2:38}?

The Bible cannot contradict itself for it is the Word of God. What we need today is a revelation from the Almighty God in order to for us to understand and dovetail every word in it correctly. Let us therefore take a closer look upon this all-time controversial issue.

The word "baptize" originated from the Greek Word "baptizo" which means to "IMMERSE" in water. For the first thirteen hundred years from the death of Christ, baptism was always performed by IMMERSION of the person UNDER WATER.

Acts 8:39 states this, "And they went both DOWN INTO the WATER, both Philip and the Eunuch; and he baptized him". John 3:23 also states, "John also was baptizing at Aeneon because there was MUCH WATER there" . "They came up OUT OF THE WATER" (Acts 8:39).

It is therefore evident from these very scriptures that Water Baptism was originally performed by "immersion" of the individual person under water.

TITLES OR NAME?

In Matthew 28:19 we can read Jesus' great commission unto His disciples saying, "Go ye therefore, and teach all nations, BAPTIZING them in the NAME of the Father, and of the Son, and of the Holy Ghost."

Now, Jesus Christ, the Author and Finisher of our faith, never told us to baptize in the NAMES, but in the N-A-M-E, (singular). The clue here is to find what NAME the Father, the Son, and the Holy Ghost possess. Take note that the word "Father" is not a NAME. "Son" is not a NAME either; neither is the Holy Ghost a NAME. These are but TITLES of the ONE true GOD.

If we trace God's Name back in the Old Testament, we will find that God the FATHER was always called the "LORD", capital "L-O-R-D".

In the New Testament, we find that "JESUS" was the name given to the SON of God.

In this our age, the dispensation of grace, when the Holy Ghost was given since the Day of Pentecost, He is called the "CHRIST" or the "Anointing" of God.

We can now therefore conclude from these basis that the TITLES of "Father, Son and Holy Ghost" refer to only one compound NAME, which is the only Name which was given on earth whereby man must be saved (Acts 4:12) - and that NAME is nothing else but the NAME of the "LORD JESUS CHRIST", the complete NAME of GOD.

We can read all throughout the Bible that ALL of Jesus' disciples used His NAME in Water Baptism {Acts 2;38; Acts 19:1-5; Acts 10:46-48; Acts 8:14}.

NEVER can we find in the entire pages of the Bible where anybody was ever baptized using the TITLES of Father, Son and Holy Ghost. Look it up for yourself and you'll NEVER find one. There's a million dollar reward today for anyone who can find one verse that states just that.

The apostles understood that baptism in those TITLES was not a LITERAL command, just as when Jesus told them, "Except you EAT My FLESH and DRINK my BLOOD, you have NO Life in you". Nowhere in the Bible can we find that they literally ATE the flesh of Jesus nor DRANK his blood. Literally eating Jesus'

FLESH and literally DRINKING His BLOOD would make them cannibals and vampires if such command was followed to the letter. But the thing is that it was revealed unto them that eating His Body means "partaking of His Word" and drinking his Blood meant "receiving His Atoning sacrifice" into their lives. In Water Baptism, It was revealed also unto them WHO really was the Father, the Son and the Holy Ghost, and what the NAME of God really was. "Lord Jesus Christ", that's the complete Name of God.

THE APOSTLES HAD A CORRECT REVELATION

Apostle PETER, having been given the keys to the Kingdom, commanded the JEWS, saying, "REPENT everyone of you and BE BAPTIZED in the NAME OF JESUS CHRIST for the remission of sins" (Acts 2:38) "and you shall receive the gifts of the Holy Spirit."

The same FORMULA was used by Saint PAUL. Paul himself REBAPTIZED the disciples of John the Baptist (Acts 19:1-5) in this same manner, saying, "Have ye received the Holy Ghost SINCE you believed? They said, 'We know not whether there be any Holy Ghost.' Paul said, "How was you baptized?" They said,' We've been baptized unto John.' Then said Paul, "John verily baptized with baptism of repentance, saying to the people that they should believe on Him that should come after him, that is on CHRIST JESUS." WHEN THEY HEARD THIS, they were baptized in the NAME of the LORD JESUS" .

PETER AND JOHN did the same to the SAMARITANS as well in Acts 10:48," And he commanded them to be BAPTIZED in the NAME of the LORD JESUS".

The GENTILES who were in the house of Cornelius who first received the Gospel were also baptized in this same manner {Acts 10:46-48} , "For they heard them speak with tongues, and magnified God. Then answered PETER, "Can any man forbid water, that these should not be baptized, which have received the Holy Ghost as well as we? AND HE COMMANDED them to be BAPTIZED in the NAME of the LORD JESUS".

ALL true believers in the Bible, both Jews, Gentiles and Samaritans, were ALL baptized in the NAME of JESUS CHRIST, for that is the genuine and Biblical way of doing it. What about you?

It was the Roman Catholic Church that brought forth such false baptism of sprinkling, and changed it from the Name of the Lord Jesus Christ to Father, Son, Holy Ghost after the year 325 A.D. Majority of her daughters, the Protestant churches, had taken the same dogma till this day and are observing blindly the same formula without realizing it so. (Read historical facts at the bottom).

WOULD YOU SAY PETER AND PAUL WERE WRONG?

No. These apostles knew what most religious leaders of today FAIL to recognize.

First: That the NAME of the Lord Jesus Christ is the FAMILY NAME of all Christians both in heaven and on earth {Read Eph.3:15}.

Second: There is NO OTHER NAME under heaven whereby we must be SAVED only in the Name of JESUS {Acts 4:12}.

Third: That the FULLNESS of the Godhead dwelleth BODILY in CHRIST {Col. 2:9}.

And fourth: That BAPTISM must be performed in the NAME of the CRUCIFIED (Read 1 Cor. 1:13).

The Bible tells us that "Whatever you DO in word or in DEED, do ALL in the NAME of the LORD JESUS CHRIST" (Col. 3:17). JESUS even taught us that "REPENTANCE and REMISSION of sins should be preached in HIS NAME, beginning at Jerusalem, unto the uttermost parts of the world" (Luke 24:47).

THREE TITLES TO ONE NAME

Father, Son and Holy Ghost are THREE TITLES. Yet there is only ONE NAME. It was revealed unto the apostles that salvation alone goes in the NAME of JESUS CHRIST (Acts 4:12).

The Bible teaches that there is NO salvation in any other name, title or places, ONLY in the NAME of JESUS CHRIST (Acts 4:12). Yet He is the "Rose of Sharon", "Lily of the Valley", "Morning Star", "Alpha and Omega" - HE IS ALL THESE THINGS, yet there's NO SALVATION in any of these titles; ONLY IN THE NAME OF JESUS CHRIST.

God has so many TITLES: "Our Righteousness", "Our Peace", "Ever-Present", "Our Father", "Our King", "Prince of Peace", "Son", and "Holy Ghost". BUT He has ONLY ONE HUMAN NAME, and that NAME is JESUS - by which Name every knee shall bow and every tongue shall confess that He is King of kings and Lord of lords.

Everyone, therefore, that is BAPTIZED with the TITLES of Father, Son and Holy Ghost is baptized in NO NAME AT ALL. They are TITLES like Minister, Reverend, Doctor, whatevermore, Father, Son, Daughter, Wife - TITLES.

You may say it does not make a difference. Then try putting your TITLE on your check and not your NAME, and see whether the BANK would encash it - say, "I sign this check in the name of the Husband"... That just make sense as it would to disbelieve God's Word when the revelation is laying right here before your eyes.

That NAME is the Password to heaven. It is also the KEY to all the heavenly blessings and supernatural gifts that God has given to the church. "In my NAME you shall cast our devils, In My NAME you shall speak with new tongues, in My NAME you shall lay hands on the sick and they shall recover" (Mark 16:17-18). "If ye shall ask any thing in my NAME, I will do [it]." (John 14:14).

WHAT ABOUT MATTHEWS 28:19?

The above-given Scriptures (Book of Acts) are not given to refute Matthew 28:19 where Jesus told the apostles to baptize in the NAME of the Father, of the Son, and of the Holy Ghost. They merely show HOW the command was interpreted and obeyed by the disciples in the entire Bible.

Now if you have not been baptized in the NAME of the LORD JESUS CHRIST yet, YOUR BAPTISM IS WRONG. You have to be REBAPTIZED AGAIN in the NAME of Jesus Christ in order for you to receive the Spirit of God.

Acts 2:38 plainly says, "REPENT, everyone of you, and BE BAPTIZED in the NAME of JESUS CHRIST for (What?) the REMISSION OF SINS - (You are still in your sins if you are not baptized in the NAME of the LORD JESUS CHRIST for no other Name is given whereby we must be saved), "AND YOU SHALL RECEIVE THE GIFT OF THE HOLY GHOST".

GOD IS CALLING ON YOU TODAY, SINCERE CHRISTIAN, to be restored back to the original faith that was once delivered to the saints. As Romans 8:30 says, "Whom He did predestinate, them He also CALLED: and whom He called, then He also justified: and whom He justified, them He also glorified."

If you are God's predestinated seed, you will recognize this Message to be the Truth. And you will not wait long until you are baptized in the NAME of the LORD JESUS CHRIST. Get right with God now while mercy and grace is upon your reach. "Obedience is better than sacrifice" {1 Samuel 15:22}.

Find a church wherein they believe this End Time Message and be baptized in the NAME of the JESUS CHRIST for the assurance of your salvation.

"Everywhere in the oldest sources, it states that baptism took place in the Name of Jesus Christ." "The Early Church always baptized in the Name of the Lord

Jesus until the development of the Trinity Doctrine in the 3rd Century." {Pp. 53}.

"Christian Baptism was administered using the words "In the Name of Jesus". The use of a Trinity formula of any sort was not suggested in the early church history. Baptism was always in the Name of the Lord Jesus until the time of Justin Maryr when triune formula was used."

THE TRUTH ABOUT INFANT BAPTISM

Most Christian churches today baptize babies by sprinkling water on them and calling it "infant baptism". But nowhere in the Bible can we find where the Apostles of Jesus ever baptized babies. Infant Baptism is not a Biblical teaching; it is a dogma of the Roman Catholic Church. There's no baby that was ever sprinkled in the Bible.

In the Old Testament, we will find that the the high priest circumcised the babies on the 8th day. Leviticus 12:2-3, "Speak unto the children of Israel, saying, If a woman have conceived seed, and born a man child: then she shall be unclean seven days; according to the days of the separation for her infirmity shall she be unclean. And in the eighth day the flesh of his foreskin shall be circumcised."

But in the New Testament, the only way the apostles dedicated the babies unto God is by bringing the little ones to the Lord Jesus. Jesus lifted them up in His hands, and blessed them, saying, "Suffer little children to come unto Me, and forbid them not: for of such is the Kingdom." {Matt. 19:13-15; Luke 18: 15-17}. Thus, this is the correct Biblical formula for dedicating babies unto the Lord.

Water Baptism is a confession that an inward work of grace has been done. Yet little infants has no knowledge of sin and they know not how to repent. But of course, the baby is borned in sin, shaped in iniquity, comes to the world speaking lies, and they're sinners by nature.

But when Jesus died at the cross, He died to take away the sins of the world. And when a baby becomes a human being and is born into this world, they have no sin of their own. The Blood of Jesus Christ already atones for the baby's sin. And therefore they have no repentance to be done and no water baptism is required of them, not until they reach the age of accountability.

The baby comes to the age of accountability between the age of 12 to 13 years old. During such age, the child knows already what's right and wrong. Therefore, it's the proper time for him or her to repent for what he/she has done. And when he/she repents, then's that's the time to undergo water baptism (Acts 2:38 - "Repent and be baptized..") by immersion.

"A little child, no matter what kind of a parent it's got, how sinful they are, that wouldn't make any difference, for the Blood of Jesus Christ cleanses its sin. That baby cannot repent. It doesn't know how to repent. It has no reasons of being here of its own. It can't tell you why it's here. But God sent it here. And the Blood of Jesus Christ cleanses it the very moment that it comes into the world, and it's until it's the age of accountability, and then it knows right and wrong. And then what it does, it's got to repent for what it knows that it's done wrong. And then the blood of Jesus Christ cleanses and makes an atonement for that child. If it dies, he perfectly goes right into the Presence of God.

And if it was born from the most sinful parents in the world, until it's the age of accountability where it knows right and wrong, and then what it does from then on, it's got to be forgiven for that. It's got to ask its own repentance from then on." And now, because a baby is, 'far as sin, it has none. Jesus died to take the away the sins of world, and the baby has done no sin. Only it was--it's a sinner. It's borned in sin.

But, when Christ died at Calvary, He took away the sins of the world, and the baby is not responsible until it becomes the age of accountability. And any little baby, no matter how sinful the parents are, as soon asthe baby dies, it goes straight to the arms of Christ. See?

Because He paid the price. No matter if it was a baby borned in sin, and by adultery, or whatever it is. Makes no difference at all. That baby is safe with Christ, because He died to take away the sins of the world. And, when it gets old enough now that it's done personal sin, then it has to repent for what it has done. But it has no personal sin until it's old enough to commit sin, to know which is right and wrong!

IS HELL EVERLASTING OR ETERNAL?

*I*t is written:
And fear not them which kill the body but are not able to kill the soul: but rather fear him which is able to destroy both soul and body in hell.

Matthew 10:28. .and death and hell delivered up the dead which were in them: and they were judged every man according It is written, And fear not them which kill the body, but are not able to kill the soul: but rather fear him which is able to destroy both soul and body in hell. Matthew 10:28.

…and death and hell delivered up the dead which were in them: and they were judged every man according to their works. And death and hell were cast into the lake of fire. This is the second death. And whosoever was not found written in the book of life was cast into the lake of fire. Rev.

20:13-15 For centuries churches have thought the concept that after the Great White Throne Judgment all sinners go to a burning Hell and remain there for eternity, experiencing the torments of burning fire. **But is this what the Scriptures actually teach** concerning the end of, not just the dyed-in-the-wool sinners, but the religious unbelievers in the whole Word of God and form of godliness church goers, etc.? **Let's take another journey through the Scriptures** to get a better understanding of "Hell" versus the "Lake of Fire". When the Bible speaks of "Hell" and the "Lake of Fire" **is it speaking of one and the same place?** I can assure you that the Bible is clear in this matter. It's not a "riddle" but a Spiritual "revelation", clearly taught in the Bible.

We will be challenged to accept the Word of God or the word of denominational and/or non-denominational churches which teach the doctrine of an "eternal" burning "hell" in which humans experience the torment of a fire that does not consume them.

To understand **what the Bible teaches** regarding the end of those judged unworthy to enter into the glories of heaven, Bible teachers and preachers are **duty bound** to "study the Scriptures" and **be honest** in what it teaches - staying with the WORD of God and not the Church.

To stay with the Church teaching when we know that it is false then we become "two-fold more the child of Hell" . While waiting for us to finish an in-depth study of Hell, consider these thoughts:

Revelation 2:11, *"He that hath an ear let him hear what the Spirit saith unto the churches. He that overcometh shall not be hurt of the second death."*

This message is to comfort us today even as it has comforted our brethren all down through the ages. But in this Age when the Mystery of God is being finished, we have a greater understanding of Hell and the "Second Death". Here in this Scripture He tells us that the second death will not hurt us. **We** all know that the second death is the lake of fire. Revelation 20:14 says: *"**And death and hell were cast into the** lake of fire. This is the second death. " Revelation 20:15 tells us that ".* ..whosoever was not found written in the book of life was cast into *the lake of fire."* Let's think on these things for a few minutes. To many who have been taught to believe that "Hell is Eternal", what I say will seem like strange doctrine - but what I say will be absolutely Scriptural.

But on the authority of the Word of God I can deny the doctrine that the unbeliever goes to an eternal hell and burns there eternally. **In the first place, hell, or the lake of fire, or whatever you want to call it is not eternal**. Eternal is something which had NO BEGINNING and NO END; therefore, how can Hell be Eternal since it had a BEGINNING?

In *Matthew 25:41,* it says that *"everlasting fire was prepared for the devil and his angels. "* Now if it was prepared, then it wasn't without a beginning. If it had a beginning, then it can't be eternal. Of course, you might stumble over the idea of the word 'everlasting.'

But that word means "from the ages to the ages" and has different meanings attached to it. In I **Samuel 3:13-14,** God told Samuel that He was going to judge the house of Eli forever, and that they would offer no more sacrifices "forever" as His priests. And in **II Kings 2:27**, Solomon thrust out the last descendants of Eli from the priesthood. That was four generations or so later. Now you can see that "everlasting" does not compare with what is "eternal", or that which had no beginning or end. Here in this case the word everlasting means *"to the vanishing* *point."* That is what happened. They vanished. Look at the word, "destruction" over in II Thessalonians 1:9, "Who shall be punished with everlasting destruction." In the Greek, "destruction" positively means annihilation. And the word, "destruction", does NOT mean destroying. Now "destroying" means something going on and on in decay. So what can everlasting annihilation mean? It doesn't mean to keep on annihilating, or that would make the word "destroying", instead of "destruction". It means to destroy to the ending point. End it.

You might wonder now, when you can use that word, "eternal", and not use it the way we have been taught. That is easy. When it applies to God it means to be without beginning or end, and ever enduring and never ceasing. And when you talk of eternal life you have that in mind which is the life of God. "This is the record, that God has given us eternal life, and that life is in the Son. He that hath the Son hath life." Now then, only sons of God have life eternal, the kind that never had a beginning, but always was. That is right. You have something in you right now that is eternal--without beginning or end. It is the Spirit of God. It is a part of God Himself.

It is the life of God. Now if a sinner is going to go to hell and then suffer the same as you are going to heaven and enjoy heaven, then he has the same kind of life you have already. Well, then there might be those who say eternal life signifies the welfare of the children of God. It is their welfare and enjoyment that is at stake. On the other hand the sinner goes to his punishment, so that we can reduce the second death to a matter of punishment and place. Eternal life means heaven, and eternal punishment means hell. You would be surprised at the men who have been exalted as theologians that believed that.

But do you know what that does? It makes eternal life a matter of geography instead of a Person. Eternal life is God,--the Lord Jesus Christ. How anyone could believe such a thing, that eternal life is a matter of place, is more than I know. It makes me stagger to think of it. **No sir. There is only one kind of eternal life. God has it. If we have God, we have eternal life in and through Him**. So you see, that word eternal, or everlasting, can be applied in various ways, but when it applies to God,

He being what He is, it has one meaning. It is the duration of God. You can't apply it like that to any other thing. God alone is eternal, and because He lives, we live with Him. **Now don't let anyone say that I don't believe in a lake of fire and in punishment. I don't know how long it will last, but it will eventually be removed**. In Revelation 21:8, it says that those sinners mentioned will have their part in the lake of fire. But the true interpretation of the word is not 'part' but it is 'time.' See, there you have it. So the wicked shall be cast into hell (Hades or the grave) and hell into the lake of fire. Separated from God. What a terrible thing that will be. But with the righteous it shall not be so. They don't have to fear. They have been redeemed by God. They are in His bosom. They are the overcomers. And who is he that overcometh? He that believeth that Jesus is the Christ. Why will this overcomer, this believer escape, and go into realms of eternal life and bliss? Because Jesus paid a price to ransom us from sin. He filled the gap of separation, and we who were afar off are now made nigh by the blood.

And they will never come into condemnation. They will never be in that lake of fire. They can never be lost for He will lose none of them. Not one of the redeemed will be anywhere except where Jesus is.

And death and hell were cast into the lake of fire. This is the second death. And whosoever was not found written in the book of life was cast into the lake of fire. Rev. 20:13-15. For centuries Churches have thought the concept that after the Great White Throne Judgment all sinners go to a burning Hell and remain there for eternity, experiencing the torments of burning fire.

But is this what the Scriptures actually teach concerning the end of sinners? Let us take another journey through the Scriptures to get a better understanding of **"Hell"** versus the **"Lake of Fire"**.

When the Bible speaks of **"Hell" and the "Lake of Fire" is it speaking of one and the same place?** I can assure you that the Bible is clear in this matter. It is not a "riddle" but a Spiritual "revelation", clearly taught in the Bible. We will be challenged to accept the Word of God or the word of denomination or non-denominational Churches which teach the doctrine of an **"eternal" burning "hell"** in which humans experience the torment of a fire that does not consume them. To understand what the Bible teaches regarding the end of those judged unworthy to enter into the glories of heaven, Bible teachers and preachers are duty bound to "study the Scriptures" and be honest in what it teaches - staying with the WORD of God and not the Church. We have seen many Church members holding firm to the wrong teachings of their pastors rather than the true word of the Living God.

To stay with the Church teaching when we know that it is false then we become "two-fold more the child of Hell" . While waiting for us to finish an in-depth study of Hell, consider these thoughts:

Revelation 2:11, He that hath an ear let him hear what the Spirit saith unto the churches. He that overcometh shall not be hurt of the second death.

This message is to comfort us today even as it has comforted our brethren all down through the ages. But in this Age when the Mystery of God is being finished we have a greater understanding of Hell and the "Second Death". Here in this Scripture He tells us that the second death will not hurt us.

There cannot be an Eternal hell. Cause if there ever was an Eternal hell, then there always was an Eternal hell, 'cause Eternal... There's only one form of Eternal Life, and that's what we're all striving for. And if you're going to burn forever and for Eternity, then you'll have to have Eternal Life burning, and then it'd be God burning. You can't have Eternal hell, and the Bible plainly says that "hell was created."

And if it's created, it isn't Eternal. Anything that's Eternal never was created; it always was, it's Eternal. And the Bible says that "Hell was created for the devil and his angels." Hell was created, it isn't Eternal. And I do not believe that a person will be Eternally punished.

Matthew 25:41 Then shall he say also unto them on the left hand, Depart from me, ye cursed, into everlasting fire, prepared for the devil and his angels:

1. THE WORD-BRIDE: THE WISE VIRGINS

FIRST of all we know most assuredly that the purpose of God stands in ELECTION.

It was God's purpose to bring forth a people like unto Himself who would be Word-Bride. **She was chosen before the foundation of the world in HIM.** She was foreknown and beloved before she was ever brought forth during the ages upon the earth. She was redeemed by His blood and can NEVER come into condemnation. She can never be in the judgment because sin cannot be imputed unto her.

Romans 4:8, *"Blessed is the man to whom the Lord will not impute sin."* But indeed she shall be with Him in His throne of judgment, judging the world and even angels. Her name (each of her members) was written in a section of the Lamb's Book of Life before the foundation of the world."It's the Elected who God, before the foundation of the world, seen every one of them. And He sent Jesus to redeem that people, not the whole world... And then, Christ died to save those who God, by foreknowledge, elected to meet Him yonder without spot or wrinkle. Before the foundation of the world, God already seen you in Glory. Ephesians 5:1. God predestinated by foreknowledge.

Now, if God did that, predestinated us before the foundation of the world; and knew every one of us by name, before the foundation of the world; and He Elected us to Eternal Life; and sent Jesus Christ to redeem us; He saw us, that we might appear to His praises in Glory! How can you ever be lost? Now, if you are saved, you're saved.

If God saves you tonight, knowing He's going to lose you ten years from today, He is defeating His Own purpose; the infinite, Almighty, Eternal, in His everlasting wisdom, God, doesn't know enough then to know whether you will hold out or whether you won't. Then, when He saves you, you say, "Well, I'll give Him a try. I'll see what He does," then He does not know the end from the beginning. But absolutely God knows what He is doing. You should never worry about that. It's you and I, stumbling along. God knows exactly what He is doing. And He knew whether we would hold out, or what we would do."

The WORD-BRIDE will sit with CHRIST in JUDGMENT.

1Corinthians 6:2-3, "Do ye not know that the saints shall judge the world? and if the world shall be judged by you, are ye unworthy to judge the smallest matters? Know ye not that we shall judge angels? how much more things that pertain to this life? " Revelation 3:21, "To him that overcometh will I grant to sit with Me in My throne, even as I also overcame, and Am set down with My Father in His throne." See?

The Bride is with Christ in the throne. As she is to judge the world she has to be sitting in the judgment with Him. That is exactly what Daniel saw. Daniel 7:9-10, "*I beheld till the thrones were cast down, and the Ancient of days did sit, Whose garment was white as snow, and the hair of His head like the pure wool: His throne was like the fiery flame, and His wheels as burning fire. A fiery stream issued and came forth from before Him: thousand, thousands ministered unto Him, and ten thousand times ten thousand stood before Him: the judgment was set, and the books were opened."* Oh hallelujah, amen! It is the same scene, for the thousand thousands who are ministering to Him are the Bride, for who ministers to the husband but the wife? She is part of Him. She is in the throne. She can never be judged. Everyone in the Bride is a member of Him and He loses none.

2. THE FOOLISH VIRGINS

Secondly, there is another class. Their names are also in the Book of Life and they will come up in the second resurrection. Such are the foolish virgins and the righteous as are spoken of in Matthew 25. This class of people, also are those who do not worship the beast or become involved in the antichrist system but die for their faith even though they are not in the bride, not having been born again. But they will come up in the second resurrection and go into eternal life.

"Virgin" means "purity." They were all good people, every one of them virgin, sanctified vessels of God. But those who had oil {the Holy Spirit filled} in their lamps went in. And the others were left out. They were all virgins, everyone people that you couldn't put your finger on for anything wrong. They everyone believed in the coming of the Lord. They were ready to go meet Him, but some of them let their oil go out... Ten virgins went out to meet the Lord, all sanctified, all holy, every one of them sanctified. Five were dilatory and let their lights go out.

Five had oil in their lamps. "And, behold the Bridegroom cometh." And the five that had oil in their lamps went into the wedding supper. And the others were left outside, they were weeping, and wailing, and gnashing of teeth. Be ye therefore ready, for you don't know what minute the Lord comes. What is the Oil represented in the Bible? Holy Spirit.

The FOOLISH VIRGIN didn't know until she come back and found the WISE VIRGINS GONE. Then she was LEFT for the tribulation period. Every good teacher believes that the BRIDE goes in the translation; but. the church goes through the tribulation, but NOT the Bride.

The church goes through for purification, sure, under the sixth seal. ISRAEL does the SAME thing, for the hundred and forty-four thousands of Revelation 7, but NOT the Bride. There's... The bride's forgiven. She goes STRAIGHT to glory in the rapture. That's right. In my opinion, the last member will be caught up one of these days. It might come, and you wouldn't know nothing about it. Remember, it's a SECRET, secret catching away. He will come in an hour that you think NOT. You won't know anything about it; she will be gone, be too LATE then."

The five foolish virgins were not lost; but they were not permitted to go into the wedding supper, but they suffered persecution, and was martyred, and raised again at the general resurrection in the last day.

He separated the sheep from the goats (See?); they stood before judgment. We do not stand before the judgment. We are now standing before the Judgment. God put our sins upon Christ, and we. "He that heareth My Word (John 5:24) and believeth on Him that sent Me has Eternal Life and shall not come into the judgment but has passed from death unto Life."

No more judgment for the Church, it's taken up in the rapture, and comes back to pass judgment upon the people who did not receive the Holy Spirit. Did not Paul say that he dares any of us to take a matter to the court, to the unjust magistrate, when, "know ye not that the saints shall judge the earth?" We will set with Christ and judge, kings, and priests, and judge these people that we preached to and told them about the baptism of the Holy Ghost and they refused to receive It. Think of it. No, they were not lost, but they will never be in the Bride. They will come in the second resurrection, but never be in the Bride, to be judged according to the way they treated the Light that they received. The Foolish Virgins will have to go through the tribulation period. And the reason is that she has rejected the Atonement in Its fullness. She is a believer, a professed believer, but she will have to go through the tribulation period. She's not the Bride, but it's the church, the pure people that didn't have the opportunity, maybe, to receive the end-time message of the hour.

In some ways, they were blinded by these false teachers and false prophets, and they didn't get a chance, yet they are really sincere in their hearts. Truly God knows their heart, and here they're purged during this time. It is the second resurrection wherein the five foolish virgins come up. Notice that they were virgins. They did not have the Holy Spirit (oil) so they missed being in the Bride, while the five wise who had oil became a part of that Bride

3. THE BORDERLINE BELIEVERS

Thirdly, there are the borderline Christians such as we saw in Israel coming out of Egypt. These had their names in the Book of Life and their works written in the books. These having failed to obey God and being void of the Spirit, though signs and wonders were even amongst them, they will have their names removed from the Book of Life. Amongst this group will be the ones like Judas who though entirely void of the Spirit, but are religious, will have manifestation in their lives, and though on the books were not elected in Him. They are such as Balaam will be in that group. Judas was numbered with the twelve and actually had a part with them in the ministry previous to Pentecost. Acts 1:16-17, *"Men and brethren, this Scripture must needs have been fulfilled, which the Holy Ghost by the mouth of David spake before concerning Judas, which was guide to them that took Jesus. For he was numbered with us, and had obtained part of this ministry."* The part that Judas obtained amongst the twelve and then lost was neither inferior to the ministries of the other eleven, nor was it a devilish foreign ministry interjected amongst the ministries of the others. Acts 1:25, "That he may take part of this ministry and apostle-ship, from which Judas by transgression fell, that he might go to his own place. " Judas, a devil, lost the God given Holy Ghost ministry, and killed himself and WENT TO HIS

OWN PLACE. His name was even in the Book of Life. But his name was blotted out. Oh God have mercy!

4. THE REPROBATES

Fourth are the ones whose names have never been or will ever be written on the books. Such are found in Revelation 13:8 and Revelation 17:8, *"And all that dwell upon the earth shall worship him, whose names are not written in the Book of Life of the Lamb slain from the foundation of the world. The beast that thou sawest was, and is not: and shall ascend out of the bottomless pit, and go into perdition: and they that dwell on the earth shall wonder,* **whose names were not written in the Book of Life from the foundation of the world,** *when they behold the beast that was, and is not, and yet is."*

Jesus said that a certain group would accept one who came in his own name.

That one is the antichrist. And that is exactly what it says of them in Revelation 13:8, and 17:8. These were ordained of God but not unto election. And with this group is such that are as Pharaoh. It says of him, *"Even for this same purpose have I raised thee up.*

Vessels of wrath fitted for destruction." Romans 9:17 and 22. None of these would be placed on the records of life. I am not saying that there is no record of them. No doubt there is some kind of a record of them, but NOT IN THE RECORDS OF LIFE. Their purpose of existence has been dealt with slightly in the rest of this book but we can add four more Scriptures.

Proverbs 16:4, "The Lord hath made the wicked for the day of evil." Job 21:30, "The wicked is reserved to the day of destruction, they shall be brought forth to the day of wrath."

In 1 Peter 2:8 and it says, "Even to them which stumble at the Word, being disobedient: whereunto they were appointed." Jude 1:4 says it, too: "Who were before of old ordained to this condemnation, ungodly men, turning the grace of God into lasciviousness".

5. THE 144,000 ELECT JEWS

And out of that JEWISH bunch there are to be the 144,000, God will call with these prophets... What is it? The Spirit of Elijah off of this Gentile church will just continue right on into that Jewish church, go right on in and call Moses with him.

Hallelujah. You see it? And he'll preach the same message of Pentecost to those Jews, that they rejected the Messiah. Amen. You see it? It'll be the same Pentecostal message that these Jews will preach right over to them. And they'll hate those Jews so bad till they will kill them. And they were hated by all nations, and in the midst of the week...

Because that they raised up a great powerful 144,000. They had the Holy Ghost, and you talk about doing miracles; they did them. They stopped the heavens, and it didn't rain in the days of their prophecy, smote the earth with plagues as oft as they wanted to. They give plagues and everything else. They'll give those Romans a hard way to go. But finally they'll be killed.

Now the 144,000 in Revelation 14:4 are NOT in the BRIDE. They are called virgins and they follow the Lamb whithersoever He goeth. The fact that they have not defiled themselves with women shows that they are EUNUCHS (Matthew 19:12). The eunuchs were the keepers of the bridal chambers. They were ATTENDANTS.

Notice that they do not sit in the throne but are before the throne. No, they are not in the bride, but will be in the glorious millennial reign.

6. THE RIGHTEOUS & THE WICKED - THE SHEEP AND THE GOATS

In the great White Throne judgment there will be a separation of people.

The Book of Life will be opened and another book will be opened. *Matthew 25:31-46, "When the Son of Man shall come in His glory, and all the holy angels with Him, then shall He sit upon the throne of His glory: And before Him shall be gathered all nations; and He shall separate them one from another, as a shepherd divideth his sheep from the goats: and He shall set the sheep on His right hand, but the goats on His left. Then shall the King say unto them on His right hand, Come, ye blessed of My Father, inherit the kingdom prepared for you from the foundation of the world: For I was an hungered, and ye gave Me meat: I was thirsty, and ye gave Me drink; I was a stranger and ye took Me in: Naked and ye clothed Me: I was sick, and ye visited Me: I was in prison, and ye came unto Me. Then shall the righteous answer Him, saying, Lord, when saw we Thee an hungered and fed Thee? or thirsty and gave Thee drink:*

When saw we Thee a stranger, and took Thee in? or naked, and clothed Thee? Or when saw we Thee sick, or in prison, and came unto Thee? And the King shall answer and say unto them, Verily, I say unto you, In as much as ye have done it unto one of the least of these My brethren, ye have done it unto Me. Then shall He say also unto them on the left hand, Depart from Me, ye cursed, into everlasting fire, prepared for the devil and his angels: For I was an hungered, and ye gave Me no meat: I was thirsty, and ye gave Me no drink: I was a stranger, and ye took Me not in: Naked, and ye clothed Me not: sick, and in prison, and ye visite not: Then shall they also answer Him saying, Lord, when saw we Thee an hungered, or athirst, or a stranger, or naked, or sick, or in prison and did not minister unto Thee? Then shall He answer them saying, Verily I say unto you, inasmuch as ye did it not unto one of the least of these, ye did it not unto Me. And these shall go away into everlasting punishment: but the righteous into life eternal."

THE SHEEP ARE THOSE WHO WERE GOOD TO THE BRIDE

To further clarify this, notice specifically the words of Matthew 25:31-46. It does not say that a shepherd is literally separating sheep from goats, but it is AS a shepherd dividing sheep from goats. These are not sheep in this particular area of time (White Throne Judgment). The sheep are in His fold, they heard His voice (Word) and they followed Him.

THEY ALREADY HAVE ETERNAL LIFE AND CANNOT COME INTO THE JUDGMENT. But these do NOT have eternal life, and they are in the judgment. They are allowed to GO INTO eternal life. But upon what grounds do they enter into life eternal? Certainly not upon the fact that they already have His life as does the Bride, but they receive it because they were kind to His brethren. They are not His brethren: that would make them joint heirs with Jesus. They are NOT heirs to anything but life. They share no throne, etc. with Him. THEIR NAMES MUST HAVE BEEN IN THE BOOK OF LIFE AND NOT REMOVED. Now because of their love of the people of God they are recognized and saved. No doubt these served and helped the children of God. Perhaps like Nicodemus and Gamaliel they stood for the children in a time of trouble.

GOD'S SOVEREIGNTY

The sovereignty of God which sets forth that GOD IS GOD, and because He is God, one cannot defeat His counsels or thwart His will and purpose. But He, being omnipotent, is ruling in ALL affairs and is doing whatever He will with all His creation because all were created for His good pleasure. Therefore, as Paul says, *"If God should take of one lump of clay and make of that same lump one vessel unto honor and another vessel unto dishonor, who can be offended and cry against Him?"* That He has the right to do this on the grounds of creation alone, we cannot deny. Yet He went even further, for according to Romans 14:7-9, we have the irrefutable proof that Jesus paid the purchase price of the whole world, and therefore He can do as He wills with His own.

"For none of us liveth to himself, and no man dieth to himself. For whether we live, we live unto the Lord; and whether we die, we die unto the Lord: whether we live therefore, or die, we are the Lord's. For to this end Christ both died and rose, and revived, that He might be Lord **BOTH OF THE DEAD AND LIVING."** (Ownership; NOT relationship is meant here.) This is also set forth in John 17:2, "As Thou hast given Him power OVER ALL FLESH, that He should give eternal life to as many as Thou hast given Him."

GOD'S OMNISCIENCE

Now, if we impute omniscience to God, we must also accept that He is perfect in wisdom and righteousness. This plan of election and reprobation is the wisdom of God revealed in all ages even, as it says in Ephesians 1:3-11, "Blessed be the God and Father of our Lord Jesus Christ, Who hath blessed us with all Spiritual blessings in heavenly places in Christ, according as He hath chosen us in Him before the foundation of the world, that we should be holy and without blame before Him. In love having predestinated us unto the adoption of children by Jesus Christ to Himself, according to the good pleasure of His will, to the praise of the glory of His grace, wherein He hath made us accepted in the Beloved. In Whom we have redemption through His blood, the forgiveness of sins, according to the riches of His grace; wherein He hath abounded toward us in all WISDOM and prudence, Having made known unto us the mystery of His will, according to His good pleasure which He hath purposed in Himself, that in the dispensation of the fulness of times

He might gather together in one all things in Christ, both which are in heaven, and which are on earth, even in Him; In Whom also we have obtained an inheritance, being predestinated according to the purpose of Him Who worketh all things after the counsel of His own will."

CONCLUSION

Thus, if God has so designed that there be those whose names are placed in a section of the Lamb's Book of Life and cannot be erased for they are the names of His Bride, then we must accept that. If it also states that there are those whose names were placed in the record of the Book of Life but in the foreknowledge of God they were to fall and have their names removed we must accept that. And if there are those whose names were NEVER placed upon a record of life, we must accept that, also.

And if there are those who will enter into life eternal after the White Throne judgment solely on the grounds of being good and kind and just to the elect of God who are His brethren, then we cannot but accept that. FOR WHO KNOWETH THE MIND OF THE LORD THAT HE SHOULD INSTRUCT HIM? Rather let us be subject in faith to Him Who is our Father and live. (Extracted from the sermon SARDISEAN CHURCH. CPT.7 by Rev. William Branham)

THE "NEW BIRTH" PULLS OUT YOUR NAME FROM THE OLD BOOK

We, Christians, need the New Birth in order for us to be restored back to what we were in the beginning, the spotless, blameless, Bride of Jesus Christ. Only when we are born again can we rest assure that our names are truly written in the Lamb's Book of Life.

The new birth frees us from God's wrath and judgment.

JOHN 3:3 — "Jesus answered and said unto him, Verily, verily, I say unto thee, Except a man be born again, he cannot see the kingdom of God."

"Verily, verily, I say unto you, He that heareth my Word, and believeth on him that sent me, hath everlasting life, and shall not come into condemnation; but is passed from death unto life. " (John 5:24)

"Your name of your first nature was born and put in a Book of Life, and all your deeds were written in it, too. Everything you done under that nature were put in a Book called the Book of Life. The first life or your first union, you were joined in at birth by nature. A natural act, a natural human being associated, man and woman together, associated together in sexual affair which brought your first life here, and that's associated with sin and death. It was nature associated with death.

Your first husband that had rule over you was your nature by natural birth.

Naturally, you love the world, because you are the world and part of the world. Is that right?

Your desires were by nature to love the world which you're a part of. You're a part of nature. You believe that? And that's your natural thing. That's the reason you have to be born again (JOHN 3:3). You have to separate. You have to die to that first husband. You can't live with it. You just can't say, "Well, I'll divorce him and hang him up here till the occasion." No, sir, no writing of divorcement. He dies. The nature of the world has to die. Every speck of him has to die. You have to be reunited again with another nature.

You were separated from your first union by spiritual death. Now, you are born again or remarried again to the new spiritual union of, not your natural life of the things of the world, but of Eternal Life. That Germ that was in you at the beginning, found you. Now, your old book is gone with your old union. Now, your name has been transferred. Now, you say, "Do you mean to tell me, that my old book." God put it in the sea of His forgetfulness. You stand perfectly before God. Now, your name is now in the new Book, not in the Book of Life, but the Lamb's Book of Life. What the Lamb redeemed, not the old book of your natural union, but you're new Bride. Hallelujah!

Your new Life is in the Lamb's Book of Life, your marriage certificate (Hallelujah.) where your true eternal germ from the beginning takes hold.

Now, you're not only forgiven, but you're justified. Glory! Justified: Romans 5:1 said, yeah, Romans 5:1 said, *"Therefore being justified by faith..."* Look up the word.

The word don't mean forgiven. The word means justified. It doesn't mean you're forgiven. But the word "justified," as though you never done it. Amen. It's not even regarded at all.

How's it done? In God's Book of the sea of forgetfulness, your old book and marriage is divorced and dead and is not even in the memories of God. Amen.

You are justified. Therefore being justified... You were accused; you never done it in the first place. The old union's in the sea of God's forgetfulness. You weren't married to it to begin with. He, the Bridegroom bore your shame Himself for you in your place.

He took your place, for you were predestinated for Him to be in His Bride before the foundation of the world. The Bible said so. You are the predestinated Seed.

How did you come to do this? You were deceived into it by your first marriage, to your adulteress parent Eve. It's no fault of your own.

By your natural birth, you come after Eve, who committed adultery. That's the reason you was born an adulterous. You were a sinner to begin with. That's right. You was deceived into it. You had no... No, it ain't your fault. You never did it, because that little Germ that was in you, was to be YOU before the foundation of the world. God put your name in the Lamb's Book of Life."

You're standing completely. You never sinned in the first place. God don't even know... It's in the sea of forgetfulness. You never did it. You were accused of it by the accuser; but really from the beginning you were predestinated to be a son or daughter of God. You're standing there washed, and your old book of divorcement's put away and is dead, absolutely out of existence even in the mind of God.

You are the virtuous Bride of Christ, washed in the Blood of Christ: precious, virtuous, sinless, Son of God standing with a pure, unadulterated Bride Word that He washed by the Water of His own Blood that become flesh and manifested that He might take you, which were predestinated in the bosom of the Father before the beginning, the same as He was.

ADAM FORFEITED THE BOOK, THE "TITLE DEED" TO ETERNAL LIFE

Adam, in the beginning, was given power by God to have jurisdiction over all the earth. When God put Adam on earth, He gave him the jurisdiction over all nature, all animals, all life everywhere. Adam was an amateur god.

GENESIS 1:26-27 —"And God said, Let us make man in our image, after our likeness: and let them have dominion over the fish of the sea, and over the fowl of the air, and over the cattle, and over all the earth, and over every creeping thing that creepeth upon the earth. So God created man in his own image, in the image of God created he him; male and female created he them."

GENESIS 2:19 - "And out of the ground the LORD God formed every beast of the field, and every fowl of the air; and brought them unto Adam to see what he would call them: and whatsoever Adam called every living creature, that was the name thereof."

But Adam, our father, forfeited it to Satan. Adam lost the rights of that Book. **He forfeited it when he listened to his wife, and she listened to Satan's reasoning in the stead of the Word of God.** See, Adam lost his inheritance: the earth. Now, it passed from his hand to the one he sold out to: Satan. He sold his faith in God to Satan's reasoning.

Therefore, his Eternal Life, his right to the Tree of Life, his right to the earth belonged to him, and he forfeited every bit of it to the hands of Satan. Now, What did we lose? Well, it was given to Adam to have Eternal Life, as long as he eat from the trees he had Eternal Life. And Adam was like an amateur god over the earth. The earth was his.

Everything was given unto his hand; he could do with it whatever he wanted to.

He named it, and called it, and done whatever he wanted to. He was truly a son of God.

Now Adam forfeited the title deed to Satan. And then, Satan took the title deed. And he could not redeem his right But Satan, which does not rightfully own it, possesses and became the god of this earth. The Bible said so. Not because that it rightfully belongs to it, but he possesses it. Now, do you get it? Satan possesses that; he holds it into his hand. Death is in his hand; the earth is in his hand; the world belongs to him; every nation belongs to him; he governs and controls the whole world and everything in the world. Satan does.

The Title Deed to the earth and to Eternal Life, but when Adam forfeited it, the Satan's dirty hands could not take it; so it went back to its original Owner, God Himself. The Title deed to Eternal Life, abstract title deed to Eternal Life, when Adam forfeited it for wisdom and instead of faith, it went back to the hands of the Owner:

the Almighty God. God made us to live forever. But sin brought death to mankind. The sin of Adam and Eve brought sickness upon mankind. Without sin, there is no sickness, and no death. The human race, as we're taught in the Scripture, didn't have any sickness before sin came in. Sickness was issued in as an attribute of sin, which had to bring death. Sin is death.

JESUS, THE SECOND ADAM, REDEEMS THE BOOK FOR HIS BRIDE

1Corinthians 15:22 - "For as in Adam all die, even so in Christ shall all be made alive."

ROMANS 5:14, 16-19, "Nevertheless death reigned from Adam to Moses, even over them that had not sinned after the similitude of Adam's transgression, who is the figure of him that was to come. And not as it was by one that sinned, so is the gift: for the judgment was by one to condemnation, but the free gift is of many offences unto justification. For if by one man's offence death reigned by one; much more they which receive abundance of grace and of the gift of righteousness shall reign in life by one, the Lord Jesus Christ. Therefore as by the offence of one, judgment came upon all men to condemnation; even so by the righteousness of one the free gift came upon all men unto justification of life. For as by one man's disobedience many were made sinners, so by the obedience of one shall many be made righteous. "

I Corinthians 15:45, 47- "And so it is written, The first man Adam was made a living soul; the Last Adam was made a quickening spirit. The first man is of the earth, earthy: the Second man is the Lord from heaven."

When Jesus died at Calvary, He settled the sin question for ever before the Father, because He was a perfect Sacrifice for our sin. He was our Kinsman Redeemer. Just like Boaz, he had to be a kinsman redeemer to be able to redeem the lost estate of Ruth. And he had to make a public testimony. And then everything that Ruth had fell to him as he redeemed all of her possessions. When he redeemed Naomi, why, he got Ruth in, which is a type of the Gentile Bride, and so forth. But he was a kinsman redeemer.

Now, God, Who is in Spirit, veiled Himself in a body of flesh, which was His Son, Christ Jesus. And God was in Christ reconciling the world to Himself, and become kinfolks to human beings to suffer the penalty that He had put on the human Himself. And He became Kinfolks and a Redeemer. In other words, like this. We were put in the devil's pawnshop, and Jesus paid the price and brought us out. See? The price was already paid. Now, when Jesus died at Calvary, He saved every sinner in the world or that ever would be in the world, as far as God was concerned. Now, Jesus didn't come down and die just for me, or die just for you. He settled the sin question. But it will never do us any good until we accept it. It is by you accepting Him as your Personal Savior by faith as you receive Him, and believe Him, and then bringing fruits of your repentance.

Jesus Christ pulled the stinger out of death and sin at Calvary. By His stripes we are healed. He has redeemed us from death.

Eternal life has been restored unto us by Jesus Christ. God promised to resurrect the body of the believer in the last days. We rest in that assurance. Jesus possessed every gate. He conquered every sickness. He conquered every sin, He conquered every temptation. He conquered death, He conquered hell, He conquered the grave. He took the keys of death and hell from Satan. And we in Him are more than conquerors now. Hallelujah, amen!

The devil put us in the pawn shop, but Jesus redeemed us. He is our Kinsman Redeemer, God made flesh, Kinsfolk to us, in order to redeem us from the curse of sin and sickness, and tonight, has sent the Holy Spirit to dwell with the Church, and show signs and wonders of healing and salvation, until He returns again. THE LAMB WAS SLAIN BEFORE THE FOUNDATION OF THE WORLD "Where was Jesus slain at? At the Calvary? No, sir. **Jesus was slain before the foundation of the world. "Behold the Lamb of God that was slain before the foundation of the world." God in the beginning when He saw the sin, He saw what was to happen, He spoke the Word and Jesus was slain before the foundation of the world.**

And every person was saved, was saved (according to the Bible) when the Lamb was slain in the mind of God before the foundation of the world; you were included in salvation then. So, what are you going to do about it?" It is God. Blessed be the Name of the Lord. "It's God that worketh; not him that willeth or him that runneth, but God showeth mercy." If Jesus was slain before the foundation of the world, it taken four thousand years before it happened. But when God spoke it back here, every Word of God is steadfast. It is immutable; It is impartible; It cannot fail. And when God slayed the Son before the foundation of the world, He was just as much slain then as He was at Calvary. It is a finished product when God says so. And remember, when the Lamb was slain, your salvation was included in the Sacrifice, because the Bible said that your name was written on the Lamb's Book of Life before the foundation of the world. What about that? Then what are we going to do? It is God that showeth mercy. It is God that called you. It is God that chose you in Christ before the foundation of the world. Jesus said, "You never chose Me; I chose you. And I knew you before the foundation of the world."

There you are. So, see, that takes the scare out of you. "Oh, I wonder; if I could keep holding on, I'll make it. Bless God if I'll just keep holding on..." It is not whether I hold on or not; it is whether He held on or not. It is what He done. Not what I done; it is what He did.

And it's Christ that God looks at, not you. It's Christ. So if there's no fault in Him, how can there be fault? How can He find fault when you're dead and your life is hid in Christ through God, sealed by the Holy Ghost? *"They that are born of God does not commit sin, for he cannot sin."* How can he sin when a perfect Sacrifice is laying in his place? God never looks at me; He looks at Christ; because we're in Christ.

Now, if I love Christ, I'll live with Him. He'd never brought me in 'less He knowed. If God saved me today, knowing He was going to lose me six weeks from today, He's defeating His own purpose. Right. He don't even know the future then, if He saved me knowing... What's He want to save me for, knowing He's going to lose me? God doesn't do things and then take it back and too weak to keep His promise. When He saved you, it's for time and eternity Oh, isn't He wonderful? Now, with our confessions, our belief, our confession of our sins, believing that all of our sins are in the sea of forgetfulness.

He that will confess his sins, God is just to omit them. See? They're in the sea of the Blood of Jesus Christ, never to be remembered no more. Certainly, you do know what bleach is? Therefore, let us just take a great big washtub full of Clorox of bleach, and then take a little eyedropper, and you got one drop of black ink in that eyedropper; that is your sins. Stand right up over the tub, and squeeze it down, then look down in the tub and find it. What become of the ink? When it struck that bleach, it was so powerful it just took the coloring right out of it; It is gone, it is eternally lost. What is it? The ink itself becomes Clorox. That is what the Blood of Jesus Christ does to every confessed sin. It's forgotten; it's finished; it's divorced; it's put away. It can never be remembered against you no more. Think of it. Before Jesus was ever born, thousands of years before He even came on earth, and several thousands of years before you too ever come on earth, Jesus in God's mind died for the sins of the world, and the Book of Life was made; and your name was put on that Book of Life before the foundation of the world. That's the Bible truth. See? Your name was ordained of God and placed on the Book of Life before the foundation of the world. You were there in His attributes. You don't remember it, no, because you're just a part of

His life. You are a part of God when you become a son or a daughter of God, just as you are a part of your earthly father. That's right. The male carries the hemoglobin, the blood cells. And when that has gone in the egg of your mother, then you become a part of your father, and your mother is a part of your father also. So you are all a part of your father. Glory!

It is the elected who God, before the foundation of the world, He seen every one of the elected that are all over the world. And He sent Jesus to redeem all of them, NOT the whole world. He wanted to, but He had to make a way for those. And the only way He could do, was to send Christ, that He might become the propitiation of our sins, that those who have been elected, He could bring to Him in glory. And then, Christ died to save those who God, by foreknowledge, elected to meet Him yonder without spot or wrinkle. Before the foundation of the world He seen you in glory.

That's what the Bible said, Ephesians1:5. God predestinated by foreknowledge.

Now, if God did that, predestinated us before the foundation of the world, and knew every one of us by name before the foundation of the world, and elected us to Eternal Life, and sent Jesus Christ to redeem us, we might appear to His praises in glory, how can you ever be lost?

Now, if you're saved, you're saved. If God saves you tonight knowing He's going to lose you ten years from today, He's defeating His own purpose. The infinite, almighty, eternal, everlasting wisdom God doesn't know enough then to know that, whether you will hold out or whether you won't. Then when He saves you, you say, "Well, I'll give Him a try; I'll see what He'd do," then He does not know the end from the beginning. God knows what He's doing; don't you never worry about that. It's you and I stumbling along. God knows what He's doing. And He knew whether we would hold out, or what we would do.

YOU WERE CHOSEN BEFORE THE FOUNDATION OF THE WORLD

You see the Book actually was planned and written before the foundation of the world. This Book, the Bible was really written before the foundation of the world. And Christ, being the Lamb, was slain before the foundation of the world. And the members of His Bride, their names were put in the Lamb's Book of Life before the foundation of the world, but it has been sealed up. And now it is being revealed whose names were in there, all about it. He came to die for those that God had ordained to Eternal Life. By His foreknowledge He saw them, not by His own will. His will was that none should perish, but by His foreknowledge He knew who would and who would not. Therefore, as long as there was one name that had never yet been declared or be born in earth, Christ had to stay there as an Intercessor to take care of that name.

But as soon as that final name had been splashed in that Clorox or bleach, then His intercessory days was over. "Let him that is filthy be filthy still. Let him that is holy, be holy still." See? And He leaves the sanctuary, and then it becomes a judgment seat. Woe unto those outside of

Christ then." Your name was put in God's Book before the Lamb was slain. When His program was laid out, the whole thing, you were recognized in that program because you got Eternal Life. The word **Eternal** never did begin, and neither can it end, and you are an attribute of God's thinking before the world was ever created.

That is the only way you can have Eternal Life. And that Life, that He was thinking of you, is in you now. There is no way to separate it. And God in the beginning knew every person that would ever be on the earth at the beginning. He knew every fly, every flea, everything that would ever be. He is infinite, and He knew everything. And therefore, the day that our names on the Lamb's Book of Life, were placed there before the foundation of the world. Just think, of everyone or anyone of us that got our names on the Lamb's Book of Life. You never put it there; and no preacher never put it there; neither your church put it there; but God put it there. And when did God do it? It is written in the Blood of the Lamb. There is not enough ink remover, or whatever it is, in the world to get it out of there. God put your name on the Book of Life at the foundation of the world, the Bible said. We are just nothing. You never had anything to do with it; I never had anything to do with it; God, Himself, did it at the foundation of the world when He slew the Lamb. Oh glory, amen! By foreknowledge He knew that Christ would be here, and He was called the Lamb of God, slain from the foundation of the world. And the beast will deceive all that dwells upon the earth whose names are not written in the Lamb's Book of Life from the foundation of the world. See?

Now, there's so many fish in that lake, and when the last one's brought out, that's the end of it. Now, a preacher he just throws in the net; he pulls. In that great net, the Bible teaches, he brings in everything. He brings in water spiders, frogs, snakes, lizards, terrapins, tadpoles, and fish.

Now, it's not for me to determine or to judge, to say which is fish and which is tadpoles. You watch a Gospel message go forth. Many will come up around the altar. Sure, the net's got them. Just a little bit they will be an old Brother Terrapin will stick his head up to say, "I just didn't believe it in the beginning." He was a terrapin to start with; that's all.

And the snake will say, "You know, there's just something about that old holy-roller stuff I can't stand." It is Snake to begin with. And the old water spider starts plop, plop, plop, clung, clung, going back. It was that to start with.

When the net went over them, they were that. But the fish was fish when the net went over it too. God is the only One to determine." The elect cannot be deceived! It is impossible! They were elected and their names put on the Book of Life before the foundation of the world when the Lamb was slain. Now, who it is, I don't know. See? But the Lamb was slain before the foundation of the world, and the antichrist will deceive all upon the earth whose names were not written in the Lamb's Book of Life from the foundation of the world.

THE BOOK OF REDEMPTION:

The Book of Revelation shows us that the Lamb's Book of Life has been sealed with seven seals, holding the hidden mysteries of God that needed to be revealed in these last days. Such a Book is the "Abstract Title Deed" to the earth and contains the NAMES of the Bride of Jesus Christ who needed to be called out in these last days by the seventh angel messenger of Revelation 10:7.

JOHN THE BELOVED HAD A PREVIEW OF THE BOOK:

John the saw the redeemed in the Book which was claimed by the bloody Lamb from the One sitting on the throne. Revelation 5:1-10. *"And I saw in the right hand of him that sat on the throne a BOOK written within and on the backside, sealed with seven seals. And I saw a strong angel proclaiming with a loud voice, Who is worthy to open the BOOK, and to loose the seals thereof? And no man in heaven, nor in earth, neither under the earth, was able to open the BOOK, neither to look thereon. And I wept much, because no man was found worthy to open and to read the BOOK, neither to look thereon. And one of the elders saith unto me, Weep not: behold, the LION of the tribe of Juda, the Root of David, hath prevailed to OPEN the BOOK, and to loose the seven seals thereof. And I beheld, and, lo, in the midst of the throne and of the four beasts, and in the midst of the elders, stood a LAMB as it had been slain, having seven horns and seven eyes, which are the seven Spirits of God sent forth into all the earth. And*

HE came and took the BOOK out of the right hand of him that sat upon the throne. And when he had taken the BOOK, the four beasts and four [and] twenty elders fell down before the Lamb, having every one of them harps, and golden vials full of odors, which are the prayers of saints."

And they sung a new song, saying, Thou art worthy to take the BOOK, and to open the seals thereof: for thou wast slain, and hast redeemed us to God by thy blood out of every kindred, and tongue, and people, and nation; And hast made us unto our God kings and priests: and we shall reign on the earth."

We can see that this Book was sealed with seven seals. But then a bloody Lamb claimed the Book from the One sitting on the throne. Now, that was our Kinsman Redeemer, Jesus Christ the Lamb of God. Unto Him is handed down the seven sealed Book of redemption from the original Owner, Almighty God. When we lost it at the garden of Eden, through Adam, it went back to the original Owner. But there's been a poacher on the land, a squatter; that's Satan. This earth don't belong to him; it belongs to God. But now the Title Deed is being handed back to us again by God. Jesus had defeated Satan and had confiscated from him the keys of death and hell. Amen, and amen.

This seven-sealed Book is our title deed to our redemption. It's the title deed and Jesus Christ, the Lamb of God breaks the seals, reveals, and gives His inheritance back to His people. He gives the inheritance that He inherited by becoming Kinsman Redeemer, and freely gives it out to us. It all belonged to Him. He was the One who redeemed it. But instead of keeping it to Himself, He gives it back to the people. That's His love for us. Its redemption means all legal possession to all that was lost by Adam and Eve are restored back unto us. Its legal possession to the abstract deed, title deed of Eternal Life means that you possess everything that Adam and Eve lost. That book is title deed to redemption of the whole heavens and earth.

THE MIGHTY ANGEL BRINGS DOWN THE OPEN BOOK UPON THE EARTH

In Revelation 10, we then see a Mighty Angel carrying this **OPEN BOOK** upon the earth. This mighty angel delegated to the 7th angel of Revelation 10:7 to fulfill the final commission of revealing the mysteries contained in those seven-seals upon God's people.

Revelation 10:1-10 And I saw another mighty angel come down from heaven, clothed with a cloud: and a rainbow was upon his head, and his face was as it were the sun, and his feet as pillars of fire: 2 And he had in his hand a little book open: and he set his right foot upon the sea, and his left foot on the earth, 3 And cried with a loud voice, as when a lion roareth: and when he had cried, seven thunders uttered their voices.

And when the seven thunders had uttered their voices, I was about to write: and I heard a voice from heaven saying unto me, seal up those things which the seven thunders uttered, and write them not.

And the angel which I saw stand upon the sea and upon the earth lifted up his hand to heaven,

And sware by him that liveth for ever and ever, who created heaven, and the things that therein are, and the earth, and the things that therein are, and the sea, and the things which are therein, that there should be time no longer:

But in the days of the voice of the seventh angel, when he shall begin to sound, the mystery of God should be finished, as he hath declared to his servants the prophets.

And the voice which I heard from heaven spake unto me again, and said, Go and take the little book which is open in the hand of the angel which standeth upon the sea and upon the earth.

And I went unto the angel, and said unto him, Give me the little book. And he said unto me, Take it, and eat it up; and it shall make thy belly bitter, but it shall be in thy mouth sweet as honey.

And I took the little book out of the angel's hand, and ate it up; and it was in my mouth sweet as honey: and as soon as I had eaten it, my belly was bitter.

RECEIVING THE HOLY GHOST:

The first step to receiving the Holy Ghost is "Obedience" to the Will and WORD of God. "Man shall not live by bread alone, but by EVERY WORD that proceedeth out of the mouth of God." IN DOING THIS, YOU MUST BE WILLING TO: 1. Repent of our sin or unbelief. 2. Be Baptized or "RE-BAPTIZED" according to Acts 2:38 -39 in the NAME of the Lord Jesus Christ. If we sincerely do this - YE SHALL receive the gift of the Holy Ghost.

Repent, and be baptized every one of you in the name of Jesus Christ for the remission of sins, and ye shall receive the gift of the Holy Ghost. For the promise is unto you, and to your children, and to all that are afar off, even as many as the LORD our God shall call." When discussing "HOW" to receive the Holy Ghost we cannot overlook Acts 10:44-47. Right here we find the record of the first time the Holy Ghost fell on the Gentiles. Verse 44 states, "While Peter yet spake these words the Holy Ghost fell on all them which heard the Word. The Holy Ghost fell on those who were receiving the <spiritual revelation> (understanding) of the WORD Peter was preaching. Verse 46-47 states, "...Then answered Peter,

Can any man forbid water, that these should not be baptized, which have received the Holy Ghost as well as we?" Take notice that, it is not a sensation; it is not emotion - but it is the Life of Jesus Christ in you, producing the 'virgin birth' in you by His Word and quickening the Word to your understanding.

To begin with, the Baptism of the Holy Ghost produces a New Birth, a New Life, with a new thought, a new attitude, new motives, and objectives. It is not you that lives anymore, it is Christ (in the form of the Holy Ghost, the Hope of glory) living in you – Supreme Power in absolute control. If you have not experienced this 'changed life' then you will need to: examine yourselves, whether ye be in the faith; prove your own selves. Know ye not your own selves, how that Jesus Christ is in you, except ye be reprobates? 2. Cor 13:5.

It is not seeking to be prayed for or receiving of miracles, speaking in tongues, quoting the bible without the life of Jesus Christ demonstrated in the life of the individual worshipper but a lived life displayed from your inside to the outwards. **When I see the blood, I will pass over you. Now, it is not the chemistry of the blood, but the life in the blood displayed upon the individual worshipper. By your live on open display, you become an epistle that read of all men. See?**

The Christian faith is based solidly upon rest. A Christian is not tossed about. A Christian does not run from place to place or fuss, and fume, and worry about things. A Christian ought to come to Church with the highest of reverence. We ought to enter the Church service like real Saints of God, walk over and take our position, and keep our minds focus on Christ. We ought to forsake everything of the world. Oh hallelujah, amen!

THE INITIAL EVIDENCE OF THE HOLY GHOST:

*I*believe on speaking in tongues, but first you must have the Holy Ghost before you start speaking in tongues: and if you do not have the Holy Ghost you will be an impersonator by speaking in tongues. Yea somebody who is trying to be something that he is not. And no man should ever teach you how to speak in tongue, but we speak, as the Holy Spirit gives you the utterance. Acts 2:4. And they were all filled with the Holy Ghost, and began to speak with other tongues, as the Spirit gave them utterance. And with all due respect and reverence, permit me to say that the "Initial Evidence" of the Holy Ghost is NOT GOOD WORKS. Of course «good works» follow a Holy Ghost filled life; however one can have good works and still not have the Holy Ghost. Again the "Initial Evidence" of the Holy Ghost is NOT SCREEMING, SHOUTING, GOOD FEELINGS, EMOTION or SENSATION. And though these attributes sometime accompany the Presence of the Holy Ghost, one can still have all these experiences and not have the Holy Ghost. Likewise, the "Initial Evidence" of the Holy Spirit in your life is NOT «SPEAKING IN TONGUES». You may speak with tongues and still do not have the Holy Ghost.

Exactly right, many "speak in tongues" and still not have the indwelling Presence of the Holy Spirit in their souls. Speaking in tongues is a gift of the Holy Ghost, but is not the Holy Ghost. Your life will prove it! Is your life worthy of the gospel? As a matter of fact, Apostle Paul downplayed the emphasis on "speaking in tongues". 1Cor.14:13, 14 & 22. 13 Wherefore let him that speaketh in an unknown tongue pray that he may interpret. 14 For if I pray in an unknown tongue, my spirit prayeth, but my understanding is unfruitful. 22 ***Wherefore tongues are for a sign, not to them that believe, but to them that believe not: but* prophesying serveth not for them that believe not, but for them which believe.** SALVATION BY GRACE THROUGH FAITH...

Man is a "threefold" being - Body, Soul and Spirit. You can experience God in either one or all three of these realms. **We can have an experience with God in our Body or spirit realm and still go to Hell. Exactly right!**

But once we experience the Holy Ghost in the realm of the Soul - this is Salvation by grace! The Soul is the "control tower" of our lives. The Soul is the nature of the spirit and the spirit is the nature of the body. And we realize according to the Word of God, both the "good" and the "bad", the "righteous" and the "unrighteous" can experience the "blessings" and "anointing" of God in their lives - One unto Eternal Life, and the other unto everlasting damnation. An individual can experience one or more of the attributes of the Presence of the Holy Spirit in his/her flesh and human spirit, and still not have the Baptism of the Holy Spirit in their SOUL. *God maketh his sun to rise on the evil and on the good, and sendeth rain on the just and on the unjust." (Matt 5:44-45). For the earth which drinketh in the rain that cometh oft upon it, and bringeth forth herbs meet for them by whom it is dressed, receiveth blessing from God: But THAT WHICH BEARETH THORNS AND BRIERS [IS] REJECTED, and [is] nigh unto cursing; whose END [IS] TO BE BURNED. (Heb 6:7-8).*

In Matt 7:22-23: Jesus said "Many will say to me on that day, Lord, Lord, have we not prophesied in thy name? and in thy name have cast out devils? and in thy name done many wonderful works? And then will I profess unto them, I NEVER KNEW YOU: depart from me, ye that work iniquity." They had all these manifestations in their lives. Yet FAILED to do what God required. God be merciful! Therefore, the evidence of the Baptism of the Holy Ghost is that we will LOVE the Lord; We will manifest the «fruit of the spirit» (Gal 5:22-23). Look at the kind of person you were and then look at what you are right now and see if there is a change in you. Check out what your life were! What were your desires before, and what are your desires after? Then you know whether the Token has been applied or not. When I see the blood I will pass over you.

If you have indeed received this "LIFE-CHANGING experience" of the Baptism of the Holy Ghost. When the true Holy Spirit comes in, it is the Life of Christ that lives in the mortal, man causing you to 68 be "Spiritually minded", not just a "religiously inclined" attitude. And I say to you again, check out your relationship with God to see if you put more emphasis on the WORD of God than you do to the Church you attend; see if you really believe the WORD more than you do your Church Creeds and dogmas .

I beseech you therefore, brethren, by the mercies of God, that ye present your bodies a living sacrifice, holy, acceptable unto God, which is your reasonable service.

Now, Apostle Paul said in 1.Cor 13, that, "Though I speak with tongues of men and angels (that's both kinds) and have not Love, I am nothing. Though I have wisdom..." Now, **he's talking about having these gifts without the Giver - Love.** See? Though I have wisdom and understand all knowledge of God, all the Scripture, can put them together like any great theologian, and have not Love, which is the Holy Spirit, I am nothing." If God is a Spirit according to Jhn 8:24, what kind of spirit is God? He is **the Holy Spirit**. See? Oh hallelujah, And God is Love. Now Satan can impersonate any of those gifts. He can impersonate anything because he perverts. Sin is righteousness perverted. So you can have any of the gifts of God without having God.

HOW DO YOU KNOW WHEN YOU HAVE THE HOLY GHOST? The evidence of the Holy Ghost is he who can believe the Word. So there is the genuine evidence of the Holy Ghost. Because in John 14:26 Jesus said, When He, the Holy Ghost is come upon you, He will reveal these things to you that I have taught you, and will show you things to come.' (Jhn 16:13-14).

Now speaking in tongues is a gift of the Holy Ghost (I Cor. 12:4-11). Divine healing is a gift of the Holy Ghost. They are no evidence of the Holy Ghost. See? You cannot rely upon that. You can't rely upon the fruit of the Spirit, because the first fruit of the Spirit is love.

Many are so confused about the evidence of the Holy Ghost. Because we do know that Satan can impersonate any kind of a gift that God has given us, but he cannot take the Word. That is where he failed in the Garden of Eden. That is where he has always failed.

"Though I speak with tongue of men and angels and have not charity, it profits me nothing." (I Cor. 13:1-13). So those things don't mean that you have the Holy Spirit. But when He, the Person, the immortal Spirit of Christ becomes your personal Savior, and changes you, and throws your views right straight into Calvary, to this Word, something's happened. Yes, sir. Something has happened. No one will have to tell you about it; you'll know it when it happens. The problem is that people go after the gift instead of the Giver.

The evidence of the Holy Ghost is the fruit of your Spirit. Jesus said so, "By their fruit you shall know them." (Matt. 7:16-20). "And the fruit of the Spirit is love, joy, peace, long-suffering, goodness, peace, gentleness, meekness (Gal. 5:22). And the fruit of the enemy is enmity, hatred, malice, strife, and so forth; that's the fruit of the enemy." (Gal. 5:19-21). So, you can judge by the way you're living, where you're standing with God.

If your whole heart is in love with Him, and you love Him and are gentle, and live with Him daily, you know you've passed from death unto Life (John 5:24). If it isn't, and you're otherwise, you're just impersonating a Christian. So, there's nothing you can say is the evidence of the Holy Ghost, unless it's your life that you live.

The evidence of the Holy Ghost, there it is. When life will line up in agreement with the Word of God in every respect, it shows you've drawn your life through God's Filter. That is when God is revealed to you and you believe it. Now, when you get the Dynamics (the Holy Spirit), you have been quickened from mortal to immortality (Eph. 2:1-7). It makes the whole body come subject to the Word. **It will make you act different, look different, live different; it will just make you a different person.**

The Lamb's Book of Life

God is the Author of Life and Man's life, is recorded in a Book in heaven which consists of two parts: one section is called the "**Book of Life**" and the other section is called the "**Lamb's Book of Life**".

Every person that was ever born and will ever be born, man or woman, boy or girl, good or bad, rich or poor, righteous or wicked, are all written in the Book of Life, with the **exception** of the **reprobates** who are spoken of in **Rev13:8,** thus *"And all that dwell upon the earth shall worship him* (the beast) *, whose **names are not written in the Book of Life** of the Lamb slain from the foundation of the world. "*

All who are listed in the **Book of Life** will have to face judgment in the General Resurrection Day and will be judged according to the works that they have done in their body. **Heb 9:27** says, *"And as it is appointed unto men once to die, but after this the judgment. "* **Revelation chapter 20:12b** also makes it plain -*"And the dead were judged out of those things which were written in the books, according to their works"*.

The names of people who are written in the Book of Life can remain in there or be blotted out depending on their attitudes and subjection towards God's laws and statutes.

Generally, **the Book of Life is also called the "Book of Deeds"** which is our old record, our old union with carnal nature, before we were ever born again by the Spirit of God. **EXODUS 32:33** - *"And the LORD* said unto Moses, Whosoever hath sinned against me, him will I **blot out** of my **Book**."

REVEVELATION 3:5 - "He that overcometh the same shall be clothed in white raiment; and **I will NOT BLOT out his NAME OUT of the BOOK of LIFE,** but I will confess his NAME before my Father, and before His angels." **REVELATION 20:11-15** - "And I saw a **great white throne**, and Him that sat on it, from whose face the earth and the heaven fled away: and there was found no place for them.

And I saw the dead, small and great, stand before God; and the books were opened: and another book was opened, which is the Book of Life: and the dead were judged out of those things which were written in the books, according to their works, *And the sea gave up the dead which were in it: and* death *and* hell *delivered up the dead which were in them: and they were* judged *every man according to their works. And death and hell were cast into the lake of fire. This is the second death.* And whosoever was not found written in the Book of Life was cast into the lake of fire."

THE LAMB'S BOOK OF LIFE:

The "Lamb's Book of Life" is a special section of the Book of Life. It contains the names of the elect of God, the chosen ones, the predestinated seed, the Bride of Jesus Christ, as spoken of in Ephesians 1:4-5, "According as HE hath CHOSEN US in HIM BEFORE the foundation of the world, that we should be holy and without blame before him in love: Having PREDESTINATED us unto the adoption of children by Jesus Christ to Himself, according to the good pleasure of his will." These people are foreknown of God and are redeemed by the Blood of Jesus Christ who was the Lamb of God slain before the foundation of the world (Rev 13:8). Romans 8:30,

"Moreover, whom he did predestinate, them he also called: and whom he called, them he also justified: and whom he justified, them he also glorified" (past tense). Romans 8:33 says- "Who shall lay anything to the charge of God's elect? It is God that justifieth." **These people were ordained to eternal life and their names can never be blotted out of the Book because they were especially created to be the Queen of Jesus Christ, which is composed of a many-membered Body also known as the Church, the Wife of the King, who is destined to live with Christ in the Millennium and in the new heaven and earth.** They were foreknown of God before the foundation of the world as evident in how God addresses his son Job in Job 38:4,7 -"Where wast thou when I laid the foundations of the earth? Declare, if thou hast understanding.. .When the morning stars sang together, and all the sons of God shouted for joy?"

Those that are written in the Lamb's Book of Life will undergo the New Birth in their appointed time on earth. They will be cleansed, regenerated and forgiven and justified, as 2Cor 5:17 states, therefore if any man [be] in Christ, [he is] a new creature: old things are passed away; behold, all things are become new." Those that are written in the Lamb's Book of Life are what the Bible calls the "overcomers" and are more than "conquerors" in Christ Jesus. Only those people that belong to this group can resist the devil and can never be deceived no matter what comes and goes. "For there shall arise false Christs, and false prophets, and shall shew great signs and wonders; insomuch that, if [it was] possible, they shall deceive the very elect." (Matt. 24:24). **The elect can never be deceived because their names are written in the Lamb's Book of Life. That is clearly stated in Revelation 17:8,** *"The BEAST that thou sawest was, and is not; and shall ascend out of the bottomless pit, and go into perdition: and they that dwell on the earth shall wonder, whose NAMES were NOT written in the BOOK of LIFE from the foundation of the world..."* *"And* **ALL** *that dwell upon the earth shall worship him (the Beast), whose NAMES are NOT written in the BOOK of LIFE of the LAMB SLAIN from the FOUNDATION of the world"* **(Rev 13:8)**

THE TRUTH ABOUT TITHES AND OFFERINGS:

The reason that I chose to write about tithe in this book is to educate new converts and the backslidden brethren about their duties and obligation as they serve the Lord. And I believe there is only one way we can find out or check out the truth on what anyone claims that God has spoken. In the olden bible days, the high priest enters the holiest of hollies, once every year, not without the blood.

And in there, he makes atonement of sins for himself, and for the congregation. And thereafter, he takes off the breast plate that he hung on his chest (the Urim and Thummim). This breast plate or the Urim and Thummim has on it, 12 stones which represented the 12 tribes of the children of Israel, dotted with blood on each stone for the atonement of their sins. Read on, am trying to lay a platform to express my viewpoints.

Note that no sinner man can enter into the most inner court or holiest of holies with sin lest he drops dead and will be dragged or pulled out with a long rope tied on his waist and a bell on him too. Now if the congregation hears the bell sound, it signifies that high priest is secured and still alive. And if he comes out alive from the inner temple, it means

God has answered or accepted his prayers. And at the end of the prayers, he hangs the breast plate known as the Urim and Thummim on the door post beside the Sanctuary.

Note, am just trying to lay a platform to crystallize my message.

Now if any member of the congregation has a dream, or a vision or a Thus saith the Lord; there is only one way to confirm whether God has so spoken to him/her or not. The whole congregation will follow that dreamer or messenger and each person with a stone on his/her hand will follow the dreamer or messenger to the door post where the plate/urim and Thummim is hung and ready to stone him/ her death if he has spoken a lie in the name of the Lord. When they get to the door post of the breast plate, the dreamer will repeat/echo his message in front of the Urim and Thummim, and as he spoke, a rainbow red light will flash from the first stone to the last stone signifying that God has spoken to him/her. And the congregation will drop their stones and praise the name of the Lord. But if the red light had refused to flash through the 12 stones, it means the dreamer spoke in vain, and will be stoned to death.

But today, we do not stone them to death again but mark and avoid them, disbelieve them if what they say doesn't compare with the scriptures.

Today, the Urim and Thummim is the Word of God (the Bible).

Therefore, if any man's word does compare or dovetail with the scripture, you better forget it.

Now at this time, if I do not speak according to the Bible, please forget what I have to say and believe it not.

I am speaking or writing on a subject of THE TRUTH ABOUT TITHE AND OFFERINGS:

WHAT IS TITHE? WHO TAKES THE TITHE? WHO GIVES THE TITHE? WHY DO WE GIVE TITHE, WHERE DO WE GIVE IT? HOW IS THE TITHE MONEY MANAGED?

WHAT IS TITHE? Tithe is the 10% or 10th portion or part of our income set aside for God's service. Giving of tithe is a challenge to every true child of God including the Levites/Pastors; and that is one of the ways the devil uses to rob us from our God's given promises. God threw the challenge on us to give our tithe and reap the blessings there from. Therefore, let us throw the challenge back to God in obedience by giving our tithes and offerings and then watch what follows.

BUT THE QUESTION IS DOES GOD ACTUALLY REQUIRE OUR MONEY OR TITHE IF THE EARTH IS THE LORD'S AND THE FULLNESS THEREOF? Yes sir! God wants to demonstrate that He controls us. That He is our Lord and the Giver of all our needs. He wants us to support His work. He wants us to show our obedience to His word and to surrender to Him alone. He wants to show that He governs and controls us. To show that He needs our testimony and wants to bless us in return. Read on!

Right now, there many preachers, speaking against giving of tithes or would rather decide who to give their tithes, or even claiming that tithe has been abolished. This is misinterpreted theology, and yet claim they got revelation. That is Ichabod of giving their tithes to the wrong place of worship. Because. God does not recognize or accept tithes given to the wrong worship places. Read on!

Tithing has become one of the most controversial issues being debated in the Christian world today, and regardless of any theological interpretation or doctrinal view saying that "TITHING" is no longer applicable for today's New Testament Christians.

But the true believer will have the revelation that TITHING is still a significant part of the Christian life. The Word comes NOT to theologians, but always to God's prophets (Amos 3:7).

TITHING first appears in Genesis 14:20 in connection with Abraham and Melchizedek. Abraham, though we are no longer living under the Law: for the Law was given under Moses. But Abraham gave tithes to Melchizedek before the law was given.

Tithe is therefore never under the law for Abraham gave his tithe to Melchizedez about 450 years before Moses ever brought the law. Tithe came before the law, oh my! It is not under the law. See? The issue of tithe must be well addressed, because Tithe belongs to God. Read Gen 14:17-20. "And the king of Sodom went out to meet Him after his return from the slaughter of Chedorlaomeer, and of the kings that were with him at the valley of Shaveh which is the king's dale (valley) And Melchizedek, King of Salem brought forth bread and wine and He was the Priest of the Most High God, And He blessed him, and said Blessed be Abram of the Most High, Possessor of Heaven and Earth".

Again, the revelation from this encounter shows that Tithing **began before the law.** Before Moses brought the law, to the children of Israel, the highest on earth - that is Abraham had already given tithe to Melchizedek. (God). So how can anyone say Tithe is under the law and is now abolished? No sir, impossible! This implies that tithing actually began before Moses who gave the law about 450 years before the law.

The Lord Jesus Christ said Abraham rejoiced to see my day and was blessed. Are you catching the revelation? Therefore, all those who preach that tithe is under the law, are ignorant of the truth. It's a kuku revelation, a bald and invalid inspiration. Such preachers use Col 2:14-15 to support their message. This is purely a misapplication, distortion and misinterpretation of the scripture.

Again, notice that it was Moses that brought the law, and before he brought the law, tithe has already been given to Melchizedek by Abraham. Heb 7:1-7 **Jesus Christ is the Jehovah of the old testament and same Jehovah of the new testament hath** confirmed that Abraham rejoiced to see His day; he saw it and was glad. Jhn. 5:56. He is the I AM that Moses met in the burning bush. No wonder Jesus said, before Abraham, I AM.

Now the word Levites belong to those in the bishopric office. (If any desire the office of a bishop, see? (bishop is not a title, but an office for the prophets, apostles, evangelists, teachers and pastors). They now represent the Levites.

WHY DID GOD RECEIVE TITHE?

Tithing is a test of our stewardship over the property of God, a test of our honesty to return to God what is rightfully His, a test of our obedience to do what He told us to do, and a test of our love and desire to please Him with our lives. Tithing is a demonstration that we believe in God, and that we acknowledge that He is the provider of all material blessings. If you do not have the faith to believe that the tithe belongs to the Lord, neither can you have faith in Him to meet your financial needs. After all, if you do not believe that the tenth is His, you must not believe that the whole earth is His either. Without that confidence in His supremacy, there could be no confidence in His ability to provide our needs.

Another person once asked, **"Why does God need my tithe?"** In answering to this question, He really does not need your money or anyone else. Remember, God is the owner of the whole universe and all its wealth.

However, He has chosen to use your tithes and offerings for the expenses of maintaining "spiritual meat" in His house (Mal. 3:10). **On the first day of the week, you are to bring your tithes and offerings to the "storehouse" of your Church where you are spiritually fed** (1 Cor. 16:2). How important it is that we are faithful in our tithes and offerings, as this is God's method of funding the preaching of His Word and the spreading of the Gospel (1 Cor. 9:1314).

Read Gen 28:20-22. The issue of tithe must be well addressed because Tithe is God's money. It is so strict in such a way that, we must know why, how, and where you can give your tithe, and how it is to be handled by the ministry who receives the tithe. God has already set out the way to receive it and the way to give it. There has already been a gross abuse of it on both sides. The giver and the receiver. The Levite represents the ministry; The tithe absolutely goes to the Levites/pastors to live on or to meet the fleshly needs of the Levites. That is their salaries from God.

While the offering is for the Church administration and needs.

God is the Provider of your income, and He, being so generous only requires 10% or the 10th portion of your income and allows you to take 90% and so the 10% belongs to God.

You do not actually pay it because it doesn't belong to you, but you give it back to the Owner. We find out that so many God's children will be considering how to first pay their house rents, the children school fees, their energy or light bills etc. before considering giving their tithes.

They will be saying, oh God will understand, and by next month, I will give my tithe after solving all these financial needs. Meaning that they will truly take their 90% and as well as God is 10%, all amounting to 100%. By this act you are saying that God is placed in the second position. Again, you are saying, that you cannot be controlled by God. Of course, you are again saying that you cannot surrender to His Lordship. Note that when you hold back God's 10%, He says alright, but you will add the 5th part thereof and that's 20%. The 5th part is mathematically 100% divide by 5th which will be 20%.

And when you must have given the previous months 20%, you will then pay the present month's 10% all of which will be amounting to 30%. Lev 27:30-33.

WHY DOES THE LEVITE GIVE
THE TITHE OF TITHES?

God knows that the offerings collected are inadequate to meet the administrative needs of the Church. The congregations are not generous or do not give enough offerings. As a result, therefore the financial needs of the Church cannot be met by the offerings alone. Most believers are so generous, and also good at giving their tithes, but give little or no offerings at all. When the offering plates are passed around for collections, you even notice that the Levites or ministers themselves do neither give offerings nor give their tithes. What a shame? And on the offering plates, what do you see? You will just be seeing $1, $2, $5 or as the case may be according to their national currency denominations just too insignificant currency values.

Except for those who would like to be given a cash back exchange out of their offerings. See?

Therefore, the tithe of tithes (**heave offerings**) is used to make up the offering, when the Levites give their tithe of tithes into the offering treasure or storehouse. That is to say that after the tithes are collected, the Levites then gives out 10% of the tithes into the Church's offering box as a heave offering to make up the deficient offerings collected from the congregation.

Even those Levites who do secular jobs or their own businesses also need to give their tithes as other members of the Church used to do before the heave offerings are made. Contrary to this, a good number of the ministers, take the tithe of tithes and give it to their fellow minister friends of other local assemblies. This is a gross error! The storehouse is the local assembly where you preach or where the people are fed by the word of God. Neh13:10-12. This means that the Levite has to take the tithe or 10% of the inheritance of the children of Israel which they have given, and now give it out as a heave tithe to the Church offering box, for the growth and administration of the ministry. Num18:20-22; Neh 10:37-39. The tithe is absolutely for the Levites to feed on, as well as for the less privileged members, the widows, the orphans. The Pastors {Levites} in their discretion disburse the tithe proceeds among themselves as their take home salaries, as well as to the widows, orphans for the poor shall not cease to exist among us. I "think" this is what use it made for directly for the Church helps and government. Heb7:5-9.

THE GATE/PLACE TO GIVE YOUR TITHE:

You may give your tithes weekly, biweekly, monthly, and yearly according to the flow of your income. Deut 14:27

There is a condition of giving your tithe which most people ignore. There is only ONE place where God will receive your tithes and offerings. **WHERE IS THAT PLACE?** Deut 12:5-14

That place is in Christ Jesus!!! That is where He said He will receive your tithes and offerings. The place where

He chose to put His name. His name is Christ Jesus. Jesus said I come in my father's name and ye received me not, another will come in his own name, and him will you receive. Jesus said so.

Now there are people from other Local Churches who merely identify to certain other Local Churches for personal undisclosed reasons. And they just take the tithe which they would have given to their own Local assemblies (store house) and then giving it to external local assemblies for whatever reasons best known to them. **God cannot change in His word. Heaven and earth will pass away but not one Word of God can be broken or unfulfilled. Tithe is given and received by God's children. God does not accept or receive tithes given to wrong places. THERE IS ONLY ONE PLACE WHERE GOD WILL RECEIVE YOUR TITHE AND OFFERING. Deut 12:5 -14. That is where the token life is on the display. When I see the blood, I will pass over you.**

Not in any type of gathering place of worship, or at any gates. But only where He chose to put His name. Not a place with creeds and dogmas, or places of doctrinal errors. Most denominations know how to give gifts. They hardly would come to worship without having to give God a gift with all kinds of unscriptural persuasions of sow seed for this, sow seed for that, offering for this, and offering for that, until some will borrow to give. And of course, and truly, you cannot come to worship with empty hands. Exo 23:15, 34:20, Deut 16:17, 2Cor 9:6-8. We need to be careful about where we give our tithes and offerings

HOW DO BUSINESS BRETHREN
GIVE THEIR TITHES?

You could even cheerfully give above the conventional 10% if you are personally led to do so and as much as you can. However, you do not have to give tithe on the gross income that comes to you so you will be able to execute or complete the job or project without running short of your working capital; but giving is based on the net income. Deut 14:22-29. If you got a contract worth of $500,000 and the cost of executing the contract is $450,000. It means that your net income is $50,000 out of which you will have to give 10% of your tithe. The farmer gives tithe of his increase, and if he cannot carry it to the Church he have to turn it into cash and give the tithe.

WHO ARE THE CONGREGATION MEMBERS?

A recognized member of a local Church is one who identifies himself with the Church, been repented, baptized, gives their tithes and offerings, and supports the Church with their regular presence.

I would like to end this with a story told by one of God's Prophet, William Branham in a sermon 'watchman, what of the night" here he said a fellow brought his tithe to him; and he had seen that this fellow had a pile of bills and other outstanding debts to settle in the hospital.

So he asked the brother to hold or take back the tithe. And here the brother reminded him that the tithe is for the levites. And Branham replied yes sir, I know. And said alright, give me the tithe first, and he received it, and said to him thank you. God bless you sir. Now take it back and pay the hospital bill of your son.

He also referred to a condition when he had to pay his debt. Here he reminded his creditor that he would give his tithe as first priority and thereafter pay his debt from what remains. This shows how serious the issue of giving tithe is to every individual believer. Will a man rob God, and you ask where would a man rob God? By not giving your tithes and offerings you do not only rob God but depriving yourself from God's blessings. God challenges us to sincerely give our tithes and offerings. Mal 3:4-11. Following, the Lord Jesus called the scribes and Pharisees hypocrites; for they pay tithe of everything, but omitted the weightier matters of the law, judgment, mercy and faith. These aught ye to have done and not leaving the other undone. Mtt 23:23. See?

If we got to give our tithe, we have to get that done according to the word of God. Abraham gave his tithe. Giving of our tithes is a challenge to every true believer, and has immediate rewards.

Notice that I have been too careful in my choice of word. Never used the word "pay tithe", rather I say "give tithe" Why? Because you pay out of what belongs to you. But in this case tithe belongs to God so in return, we give our tithe because the 10% belongs to God.

THE CHALLENGE FROM GOD
ABOUT GIVING YOUR TITHES:

In closing, God challenges every one of His children to give our tithes from the least congregation member to (those in the bishopric offices) the Levites with no exception. **Now we have come far, to him that knoweth to do good and doeth it not, to him it is sin.**

Give your tithe as a necessity to invoke God's or cause God's blessing upon your lives. And the Levites/Pastors who truly are called by God, don't need to over emphasis or threaten members about giving of tithes or always talking about the tithes to their members, nor asking them to borrow to give tithes. Oh no, no indeed.

Just let them understand and to believe about the need for them to give it. Not talking about it all the time for the love of money.

HOW IS THE TITHE RECEIVED MANAGED BY THE LEVITES?

The Priests, Levites or Pastors also, give the tithe of the total tithes known as the Heave offering into the offering for the running of the Church needs.

But a true Servant of God would share the tithes with the rest of the five-fold ministry, and give to the widows, and poorer saints in their local Church

He will be reverently conscious not to live luxuriously, by buying helicopters, jets, and mansions for himself, but will be cautiously mindful that he does not stumble a soul out of the way, by such living.

He will treat the tithes and offerings as the Lord's money and will be fully conscious, knowing that he will one day give an account for it to the Lord. He will handle such funds with respect, reverence, and a lack of greed.

He will treat it as hard earn labors and will be mindful of saving and not wasting a penny of the Lord's money, which can be used for the sake of the gospel. Now it is so sad that these modern-day ministers are patterning after the rich, educated, social and religious system of organizations.

For every tithe collected, they should also give 10% of the total tithes collected into the Church's offering box as a Heave offering or "tithe of tithes. Read our message on Tithe thoroughly and you will get the bible references

ABOUT THE AUTHOR:

Bro Caleb F. Iworie

I was saved on April 1991, and with an awakening desire for the undiluted word of God: I immediately got baptized according to Acts 2:38 by immersion in the name of the Lord Jesus Christ at the Brethren Fellowship located at **Ejigbo, in Lagos-Nigeria**. Jesus said in the book of Matthew 11:28-30 Come unto me, all ye that labor and are heavy laden, and I will give you rest. Take my yoke upon you and learn of me; for I am meek and lowly in heart: and ye shall find rest unto your souls. For my yoke is easy, and my burden is light. Oh, I remember that day: it was such a memorable event as my burden was lifted with a sober feeling, seemingly out of this world rapped with unspeakable joy garrisoned with great aura of reflection and soberness. I I have a feeling of an extrovert, as an oddball. Nothing worried me anymore than feeding on the word of God. Oh God be praised! As I drew closer and closer to God, I somehow realized that something has happened to me, things were different to me, and the worldly things I loved to do I love them no more. And he kept working on me day after day. Following, in 1994, I came in contact with a devout gallant son of God, one **Bro Sylvester Roberts** {of the blessed memory}, who further expounded me by the undiluted word of the scriptures, just as apostle Paul did to those disciples in Acts 19, and brought their understanding to the way of the Lord.

APRECIATIONS/ ACKNOWLEDMENTS:

I thank you **Lord Jesus Christ** for your overwhelming enablement and your grace, that made this book evangelical outreach a success.

I must commend and appreciate the entire Bride of Jesus Christ at the **Houston Tabernacle**, especially my precious **pastor and friend, Bro Zoe Dembe** and his precious wife sis **Splendid Dembe**, for their inestimable fervent prayers and support towards this publication.

The last but not the least, my precious wife **Sis Sarah Onyelo Iworie**, my son with his lovely wife, Bro Obed Iworie and **Sis Yvonne Chukwu-Iworie**. I am so grateful to God for these brethren and pray God for their overwhelming rewards.

Now unto him that is able to do exceeding abundantly above all that we ask or think, according to the power that worketh in us, unto him be glory in the Church by Christ Jesus throughout all ages, world without end. Amen.

DISTRIBUTION CHANNELS:

This book is intended for your in-depth knowledge of God's Word and revelation.

It is believed that you prayerfully and diligently study to equip yourself with the basic fundamental truth of the Gospel of our Lord

CONTACT US:

Bro CALEB IWORIE
Email: Seedwordoutreach@gmail.com
Pastor ZOE DEMBE
Email: Houstontabernacle@gmail.com
Houston Tabernacle, 6104 Westline Drive, Houston, Texas 77036.